Ice Cream
at the Ashram

For Judy,
May your journey
be holy
Debbie

ICE CREAM AT THE ASHRAM

Holy Journey
Holy River
Holy Week

by

Deborah L. Clark

ZION PUBLISHING

Copyright © 2016 Deborah L. Clark

All rights reserved. No part of this product may be reproduced in any manner whatsoever without written permission, except in the case of brief quotations embodied in critical articles and reviews.

Scripture references are from the New Revised Standard Version Bible, copyright © 1989 by the Division of Christian Education of the National Council of the Churches of Christ in the USA. All rights reserved.

Cover photo by Deborah L. Clark

Please do not take part in or encourage piracy of copyrighted materials in violation of the author's rights. Buy only authorized editions.

ISBN-13: 978-1537761305
ISBN-10: 1537761307

For discounted bulk orders, contact the author:
Deborah L. Clark: deborahleeclark62@gmail.com

Published by
Zion Publishing
Des Moines IA

"Out of the believer's heart shall flow rivers of living water."

John 7:37b (NRSV)

For Fran, with gratitude for her love, encouragement and inspiration.

For Addison, Juan, Maria, Sister Tureeya, and the little boy on the New Delhi sidewalk, with a prayer that they—we— might find hope and peace.

✺

✴ In Gratitude ✴

Ice Cream at the Ashram is based on a week I spent at a Christian-Hindu ashram, named Jeevan Dhara, in Rishikesh, India in 2008. It includes my reflections from a three-week stay at another ashram, also named Jeevan Dhara, in Jaiharikhal, India, in 1985. In writing this book, I drew upon my memories of those two visits, aided by my journals and photographs, along with some imaginative re-creation of conversations. The people are real people; in most cases I use their real names. I am grateful for the gifts they gave me. I hope I have conveyed my deep respect for their lives.

My first trip to India, in 1985, was part of a year of independent study funded by the Thomas J. Watson Foundation. My 2008 trip was part of a pastoral sabbatical funded by the Lily Endowment for Clergy Renewal. The writing workshop that prompted me to turn my memories into this book was sponsored by the Collegeville Institute, offered in conjunction with the Massachusetts Conference of the United Church of Christ. I am grateful for these organizations that generously provided me with opportunity, inspiration, and time.

So many individuals and communities were part of my writing process as well. The people of Edwards Church, United Church of Christ, in Framingham, Massachusetts, where I am pastor, have shared their questions, struggles, and hopes with me for more than two decades. They have challenged and inspired me to keep reflecting on new ways to express our faith. Their openness to creating Open Spirit: A Place of Hope, Health & Harmony has stirred my passion for interfaith conversation. I am grateful to the warm, open-hearted people of Edwards Church and to the rich, diverse community of Open Spirit.

Maren Tirabassi worked patiently with me over two summers as I wrote and re-wrote. My life-partner Fran Bogle read numerous drafts and listened to me read still more drafts aloud. Carol Reynolds and Sarah Hubbell, friends and colleagues in ministry, offered their feedback. Mary Nilsen at Zion Publishing helped me finally bring this book to fruition. I am grateful to them all.

Table of Contents

The Saturday Before ✣ *11*
"Hints of the Holy"

Palm Sunday ✣ *19*
"Confronted by the Cross"

Monday ✣ *31*
"Reverie on the Haridwar Express"

Later on Monday ✣ *55*
"Opening"

Tuesday ✣ *63*
"The Spirit Sputters and Soars"

Wednesday ✣ *81*
"Three Hours and Eighteen Minutes"

Thursday ✻ *93*

"Immersion"

Friday ✻ *107*

"Good After All"

Saturday ✻ *121*

"A Dangerous Secret"

Easter Sunday ✻ *129*

"Ice Cream at the Ashram"

Easter Mondays ✻ *141*

"The Journey Continues"

Afterward ✻ *147*

In Celebration of Open Spirits

✸ The Saturday Before ✸
"Hints of the Holy"

The gray in his hair glistens in the fluorescent light. His shoulders stoop. Mr. Samuel, as his name badge reads, stands behind the counter, looking small and sad. I finish my conversation with Gladwyn, the energetic young Director-in-Training of the New Delhi YMCA, and I approach the desk to pay my bill.

"Are you a teacher?" Mr. Samuel asks. He must have heard me telling Gladwyn about my sabbatical plans.

"No," I answer. "I'm a pastor."

The reactions I get when I tell someone I am a pastor run the gamut. Sometimes it's a conversation-stopper, as people assume I'm judging them or wanting to make them believe what I do. Sometimes it unleashes a torrent of defensiveness, or even accusation, as people tell me how much damage the church has done—in general and too often to them. Occasionally there's a twist on "holier than thou" as they tell me how they have evolved beyond the need for organized religion, with all its dogma and rules and empty ritual.

Other times, people tell me their life story.

That is Mr. Samuel's response. His eyes lose their look of defeat as his face lights up. He forgets all about the paper work. "I've been here for 37 years," he begins. "I started here right after I got married and worked my way up. I'm the Accounts Payable Manager. I'm in charge of all the billing." Pride finds its way into his voice. And then sadness takes over. "This month I have to retire—it's mandatory."

Mr. Samuel pauses long enough to catch his breath, but not long enough for me to figure out how to respond. "I'm so worried. I don't know how we're going to pay the rent."

I'm a little worried myself. Is he asking me for money?

"And my daughter," he goes on, "I'm worried about her too. She has a big job interview coming up…. Wait here a minute," he holds his finger in the air and rushes into the back room, returning with a sheet of paper. "See, here's her resumé." I take it and read it politely. "She's a teacher," he continues. "But now the school where she is teaching is not a Christian school. Every day, after only a half an hour, she is crying." He explains that the interview is for a job at a Catholic school. "That will be much better," he says.

Now I know he isn't asking me for money, but I'm not sure what he wants me to do. Does he hope I have an "in" with the Catholic school? Finally, I realize he hopes I have an "in" with God.

"Will you call Martina?" he asks. "She needs prayers."

I'm not sure his daughter really wants a strange foreigner to call her up to pray for her job interview, and I'm not sure I want to get involved. I have a feeling he may expect me to have some magical power to elevate his daughter's resumé to the top of the pile. I wonder if he's counting on eloquent words I won't find in that moment. Besides, I'm a little out of practice, and in need of some prayer myself.

I'm two months into a three-month sabbatical from my church. I started the time off with high hopes and a grant from the Lilly Endowment focusing on the theme, "Exploring a Spirituality of Creation and Creativity." The plan involved lots of travel—much of it with my partner Fran.

I love to travel. I love the unexpected conversations on the train with someone whose life is so different from mine. I love discovering points of connection and claiming, at least for a few email exchanges, friendships that span the globe. My love for travel blossomed right here in India, when I was twenty-three years old. I spent six months here, as part of a year of independent study between college and divinity school. Back then, I soaked in the explosion of colors and smells, the abundant and diverse expressions of religious devotion, the chaos of the cities and stillness of the ashrams. When this sabbatical opportunity arose, I leapt at the chance to come back to this perplexing and fascinating country, the final leg in our journey.

By the time I am standing here debating how to respond to Mr. Samuel's request, I have taken watercolor lessons in Florida and visited the Tibetan Children's Village in Dharamsala to meet the child my congregation supports. Fran and I have explored the outrageous diversity of creation in the Galapagos Islands and the wild beauty of elephants and crocodile and boar in South India. A Buddhist monk from our hometown has taken us to ancient Buddhist sites in Sri Lanka. We have attended a workshop at the Indian School of Art for Peace and stayed at a Christian Seminary in Bangalore where an old friend is Dean of Students.

I am exhausted—and discouraged by how hard this trip has been, especially the India part. My memories of my previous trip to India have become romanticized over time; I forgot how exhausting the noise and crowds and cultural differences can be. I feel old, distressed to discover how my travel stamina has eroded over the years. We lost our luggage in the Bangalore airport; we were stranded in New Delhi because of fog that is apparently a daily occurrence; we stood in endless wrong lines in airports all over the country. Worst of all, Fran was sick from the day we arrived in Southeast Asia, and she finally made the agonizing decision to go home early. I stayed reluctantly, worrying about her.

I am lonely and tired from all the strangeness. I'd like someone to pray for me; I'm not sure I want to pray for Mr. Samuel's daughter's job interview.

He looks at me expectantly, a glimmer of hope breaking through the sadness in his eyes. "Of course," I respond, trying my best to smile. "I'd be happy to."

Mr. Samuel—"Call me Addison," he says—suggests we go into the chapel. It is a simple room, wooden pews in rows facing a small altar with a cross. Behind the table is a picture of a blond-haired, blue-eyed Jesus, looking soulfully at us.

We sit down on the front pew, and Addison immediately folds his hands and bows his head. He is ready for me to pray. I feel awkward and out of place—and unexpectedly grateful for this odd connection with this man. I pray. I pray for strength and courage, ostensibly for Addison as he faces his retirement and for his daughter Martina in her job interview, but just as much for me and my exhaustion. I pray that Addison will discover new doors opening for him in his retirement, and that Martina will discover joy and fulfillment in her work—and I silently add a prayer for doors opening to something holy or restorative for me when I really just want to go home. I pray that whatever they face, they will know they are not alone and will feel God's love enfolding them. That prayer, especially, is for me. "In Jesus' name," I conclude, "Amen."

We sit for a few minutes in silence. I'm about to get up when Addison pulls out his cell phone. "I want you to call Martina," he says, "and pray with her."

I hate praying over the phone. That intimate connection of sitting side-by-side and praying together is lost; somehow a disembodied voiced prayer feels artificial and awkward. Over the years, though, I've learned to do it anyway, and I've discovered that awkwardness is not the end of the world.

He dials his daughter's number. When she answers, he hands the phone to me. "Hello?" She is clearly expecting her father, since it is his cell phone.

"Hello, Martina, my name is Debbie Clark and I'm a pastor."

Silence. She doesn't know what to say either.

I fumble my way through my explanation. "I was

talking with your father and he told me you have a big job interview tomorrow."

"That's right…" She still can't figure out who I am and why I am calling.

"Your father thought you might like me to say a prayer with you over the phone. Would you like me to do that?"

Her voice brightens. "Oh, yes please," she responds with enthusiasm. I feel a little less foolish. I pray—mostly the same words I used a few minutes before. I can tell she is crying.

When I finish, I sit there holding the phone, listening to her sobs quiet down. She recovers enough to explain that the interview is Monday morning. "Will you come to our home on Sunday to pray with me in person?"

That's when I realize what day it is—the Saturday before Palm Sunday. It is the day before the holiest week of the Christian year.

✻ Palm Sunday ✻

"Confronted by the Cross"

After breakfast I put on my new purple *kurta* and *pyjamas*—the best outfit I have in my suitcase. I brave my way across Ashok Marg, dodging cabs and waving away the auto-rickshaw drivers who insist they should drive me across the street for a few rupees. I'm on my way to church.

In the last eight weeks, I haven't made it to church at all. There was no church service on board the ship in the Galapagos; I swam with the sea lions instead. The next Sundays found me visiting Buddhist temples in Sri Lanka, looking for tigers at a wildlife preserve in South India, and visiting the Tibetan Children's Village in Dharamsala. I rehashed the old religion versus science debates in the Galapagos, discussed the role of church and society with Christian seminarians in Bangalore, and chanted in ancient temples with Buddhist monks. But I didn't go to church.

Today I am determined to go. I arrive early at the Church of North India's English-language service and find a seat. The pew quickly fills up around me. When the children begin processing down the aisle with palm branches, we all stand up to sing, "Ride on, Ride on in Majesty."

I start to cry. It isn't the particular song. It isn't even some profound spiritual insight. It's just that I know the words and the tune by heart. My response to that opening hymn has little to do with the story of Jesus riding into Jerusalem on a donkey a few days before he would be crucified. It has much more to do with just missing home, missing Fran, missing the comfort of the familiar. When they announce that there will be a choral concert that evening, I decide to come back. Maybe they will sing more songs that will remind me of home.

I recover from my attack of homesickness enough to shake hands with the preacher after the service, and I walk toward the parking lot. This time, when one of the auto-rickshaw drivers approaches me, I say yes. I pull a piece of paper out of my pocket and show it to him. "INA Market, please." I hop in the rickshaw and settle in for a bumpy, harrowing ride as he maneuvers through New Delhi traffic.

I don't know where I am going, or what the INA Market is. It's just what Addison Samuel wrote down on the piece of paper. "Meet me there," he said, "and I'll take you to my home." I am on my way to meet Addison's family and pray with his daughter.

We drive out of the center of the city, far from the area tourists frequent. The driver takes me past massive walled compounds and makeshift homes constructed of cardboard and tarps. We emerge at a sprawling open-air market—rows and rows of broken plastic tables covered in old magazines, children's clothes, household appliances and more.

I pay the driver. He speeds away, and I wonder how I will ever find Addison. Before I can pull out my cell phone to call, I hear a voice. "Over here." Addison is standing beside a bicycle rickshaw. I go over to greet him, and he motions to the seat. I climb up. He jumps in beside me. We watch as the wiry old man on the cycle struggles to break through the inertia and create enough momentum to pull at least twice his weight.

"The auto-rickshaws don't come all the way to our home," Addison explains. We cycle out of the market and into a vast housing complex—more rows, this time of giant concrete blocks. "These ones, over here," he says, "are for 4th class workers—sweepers. They have government subsidies, and they don't have to pay any rent." We ride past a few more, and finally he motions to the driver to stop.

"This is where we live," Addison says as he pays the driver. The building looks identical to all the others we passed. We climb the stairs to the second floor, and he opens the door to his home: a concrete block inside a concrete block.

The flat is immaculate. The concrete walls are tastefully adorned with religious wall-hangings and family photos. The couch, which looks as though it doubles as a bed, has an attractive, if subdued, cover on it. The chairs are straight-back wooden kitchen-table chairs. It appears that their home has two rooms, but I can't be sure.

All of Addison's family is there, except for Martina. His wife Susan greets me warmly, "Welcome to our home, Pastor." His teenage daughter Steffie follows suit, a bit more formally, as though she practiced it in English class. "It's a pleasure to meet you, Miss." Addison speaks to his young son Steven, who rushes out the door, returning a few minutes later with a large bottle of Coke and a box of cookies. Susan carefully lays out the cookies on a plate, and puts the plate, along with the bottle of Coke and five glasses, on a tray adorned with a paper doily. We sit drinking Coke and eating cookies, waiting for Martina to come home.

"Martina will be here soon," Addison explains. "Her friend from school had a heart attack—a very terrible thing for such a young girl."

Susan jumps in. "Martina went to visit her in the hospital. I'm sure she'll be back very soon."

As we wait, Steffie tells me about her schooling.

"I just finished my O-Level exams last week."

"Congratulations," I smile at her. "Does that mean you're done with school?"

"Oh no. Now I get to choose. I'd like to study commerce." Her voice is bright, but suddenly it changes. She gets a worried look on her face, making her look just like her father. "I hope I can get in."

Addison and Susan look at Steven; apparently it is his turn. "How about you, Steven?" I ask. "What year are you in school?"

Steven looks down and mumbles, "I just took my 6th grade exams."

"How did it go?" I have a feeling that's the wrong question to ask, but I'm not sure how else to make conversation.

"Not very well," he mumbles again. Now it's time for his voice to change—from murmured apologies to a hint of defiance. "I don't like school. I think I will not continue on after this year."

Addison and Susan shake their heads. "What are we going to do?" Addison launches into a litany of worries—tuition for Steffie's dream of commerce school, Steven's apparent lack of direction, and then, again, back to money. "When I retire we will have no income, only what we have saved, and that will be gone very soon."

"You don't get a pension from the Y?" I'm a

little surprised; the YMCA in India has a strong anti-poverty focus.

"No, there's nothing, and nothing from the government either."

I think about the concrete blocks we passed, the ones for the sweepers who don't have to pay rent. What about Accounts Payable people like Addison?

"My wife," he points to Susan, "has tension and diabetes. Our rent is 3000 rupees a month, and I don't know how we will pay it next month." I do the math. It is about $75, only a little more than I am paying for a night at the Y.

"What about your church?" They had told me they were very involved at their Methodist Church. "Would they provide some help in an emergency?"

Susan jumps in quickly. "No, there is nothing like that." The Samuels, it seems, are out of options.

Yesterday, I worried that Addison was going to ask me for financial help. Today, I find myself wishing he would. I feel powerless. Hoping I won't offend them, I offer to pay for next month's rent, to get them started.

"No, no," they insist. "We just want you to pray with us." That, apparently, is the power I do have, and it doesn't feel like enough.

The conversation has run its course, and Martina still hasn't come. The family is ready for me to pray. So I do. We pray for Steffie, for Steven's exams, for Susan's health and Addison's retirement. Then we pray for Martina in absentia. As soon as we finish, Martina comes in the door. We pray again. I hope it helps.

I finish my last sip of Coke, and we say our goodbyes. Then Addison and I go out to find another bicycle rickshaw driver, who lugs us back to the market, so I can get into yet another auto-rickshaw and head back to the Y.

* * *

I am leaving New Delhi the next day, but I don't have much packing to do. Even though I'm worn out from the morning and the heat is stifling, I feel restless. After lunch I decide I will take a long walk. I get out my overly-creased street map and plot a course, heading toward the gardens around the India Gate in search of grass and trees and maybe a bench, where I can sit and write.

Map in one hand, water bottle in the other, I set off, navigating jagged sidewalks that end abruptly and cars that whip around roundabouts without warning. I pass a fancy hotel and wonder if I look too sweaty and dusty to drink tea in their lobby. Twice auto-rickshaw drivers stop and try to convince me it is too dangerous for a foreign lady to walk down that street—"Get in, get in! I'll take you to a place you can walk. Only twenty rupees."

"No," I say. "I want to walk." They drive away, shaking their heads.

I make it to the India Gate, which is surrounded by long blocks of grass and dirt paths, with a gray creek running down the center. It is crowded. Huge families gather for elaborate picnics. Laborers take a break along the banks of the creek. Some people have set up camp and seem to live there. I wander along, quickly abandoning the idea of a quiet bench to sit and write. I wait in line to use the restroom, only to watch in confusion as women in full saris walk right past me into the empty stalls. I'm wondering why they keep cutting in line. They, I imagine, can't figure out why I'm just standing there.

Finally, fortified with a fresh bottle of water from a vendor beside the gate, I begin the long walk back to the Y. I am making my way along another one of those rutted sidewalks when a little boy stops me in my tracks. Literally. He stands directly in front of me. His hair is a tangled mess; his face is coated in dirt. His clothes are made for someone twice his size. I guess that he might be five years old. Out of the corner of my eye, I can see a young woman holding a baby girl, both of them looking as desperate and bedraggled as the little boy.

The child stands in the center of the sidewalk and holds out his hand in the universal plea. "*Baksheesh?*"

I look him in the eye. My friend who works with homeless people in Boston has told me I should at least acknowledge someone's humanity by not looking away. I say "No, sorry." Then I try to walk around him.

It is almost funny—except that it is horrifying. He might as well be guarding me on the basketball court. I move to the right, and so does he. I try to fake left, but he is a step ahead of me. By now he has abandoned his *baksheesh* position and his hands are extended fully on either side to prevent me from passing. Feeling pathetic and silly and awful, I make an attempt at a break, running into the street to get around him. But he is better at this game than I am. Short of running directly into New Delhi traffic, I am trapped.

It feels as though it goes on for an eternity. Finally an auto-rickshaw driver comes to my rescue. He pulls over and yells in Hindi at the child, who disappears as suddenly as he appeared a few minutes ago. This time, I am ready to jump into the auto-rickshaw, if the driver offers me a ride. But he shakes his head and drives off, in search of a more promising fare. Shaken, I walk back to the Y.

That evening, as planned, I go to the concert at the church. It's an impressive collection of musicians, reflecting the increasingly international flavor of the city. Choirs from every Christian church in New Delhi have come together to sing a striking mix of Indian and Western music, mournful Passion anthems and joyous Easter hymns. I enjoy the pieces in Hindi, and when the English-speaking anthems begin, I close my eyes and settle in. Some of them could have been pulled out of the music library at my own church. I allow the familiarity to wash over me, as though it can cleanse me of the dirt and exhaustion and confusion of the day. I pay little attention to the words.

The final anthem in the Passion segment wakes me up. "Face the cross," the choir sings. I know they mean for me to picture Jesus on the cross; I imagine they hope I will be grateful for Jesus' sacrifice and will reflect on the gift of redemption. But all I can see is the cross I faced this afternoon. A desperate little boy with his arms outstretched to block my path. Christ crucified on a potholed sidewalk in New Delhi. I didn't want to face that cross, and I tried my best to get around it. There was no way around. The annoyed auto-rickshaw driver today saved me from the moment. But that cross is still in my face.

"Face the cross," the choir sings. I didn't know how to get around that cross—and ultimately I don't want to. But I don't know how to face it.

Fortuitously, or blessedly, the offering at the concert that evening is designated for the Church of North India's ministry with street children. I put my 500-rupee note (a big twelve dollars) in the plate with a sigh of partial relief and a prayer that maybe it will matter. It feels like too little too late.

This morning, I offered to help Addison and his family with some money to get them through a tough time. They didn't want my money; they wanted my prayers. I struggled to trust it was enough. This afternoon, the little boy wanted—needed—my money. I didn't give it to him; all I chose to offer him was my prayer. It isn't what he wanted, and I know it isn't enough.

Today is the beginning of the holiest—and also the most intense and confusing—week of the Christian year. If I was home on Palm Sunday, by evening I would have already begun trying to figure out what I might say on Good Friday about the meaning of the cross. We argue about it in seminary classrooms and church parlors. Sometimes churches split over it. One way or another, with certainty or with vague language about mystery, we proclaim that the cross redeems us.

But there is no redemption in the cross I faced on this Palm Sunday afternoon. There is nothing that can make this cross okay. The redemption will come only when little boys no longer have to block the sidewalk to be noticed, to be fed, to find hope. Maybe the redemption begins when we dare to face that cross and refuse to go around it.

✵ Monday ✵
"Reverie on the Haridwar Express"

My alarm jolts me awake. I am ready to leave New Delhi, but not this early. It is still dark as I drag my luggage down to the lobby, store my suitcase behind the desk, and lug my duffle bag out to a cab. The cab ride is much smoother than yesterday's rickshaws, and before I know it, we arrive at my destination.

Even at this early hour, the train station is mobbed. I barely open the cab door when I am accosted by a gnarly old porter with a dirt-grey towel wrapped around his head. He grabs my bag out of my hand. "Come on," he says curtly, "follow me."

Chastened by yesterday's events and remembering that I can barely lift the bag, I swallow my usual "No, I'll carry it myself." I hurry into the station at his heels, struggling to keep up. I follow him up a flight of metal stairs, jostling with the crowds coming down the same stairs straight at me. He takes me along a long grimy corridor and down the next jammed set of stairs. I rush to keep up, worrying I may never see my duffle again. Finally, he stops midway down a long platform, and I heave a sigh of relief.

"Here," the porter says. "Wait here."

This is my first time on a train in India since my stay here 22 years ago. I flash back to my terror of not hearing the announcement for my train amidst the din, not moving fast enough to get on when it finally arrives, not being able to lift my bag over my head and onto the luggage racks.

"Thirty rupees," the porter says.

Feeling grateful for a moment, I hand him a 50 rupee note and wave my hand. "Keep the change." Then I have an idea. "How much more for you to help me get my bag on the train?" I ask.

The old man smiles. "Fifty more," he says.

My momentary magnanimous attitude shrivels away to nothing. "Never mind," I say curtly, "I'll do it myself." He shrugs, pockets the 50 and leaves.

As it turns out, the announcement crackles from the loudspeaker crystal clear, the train stops with the correct door directly in front of me, and a fellow passenger helps me lift my bag onto the rack. This is a newer train, the Haridwar Express, with bright blue vinyl seats that recline ever so slightly. I settle in, push my seat back, close my eyes, and find myself thinking, not ahead to my destination, but back to a very different train ride twenty-two years ago.

On that trip, I do not allow an eager porter to carry my bag to the platform. Instead, I maneuver my pack onto my back as I get out of the auto-rickshaw. I hold tight to the grimy handrails on the stairs so the weight of my luggage won't make me lose my balance. And then I stand waiting at the platform until the train comes, afraid that if I sit down I will not be able to get my pack back on. The train, when I finally get on and manage to shove my pack into the luggage compartment, does not have bright blue vinyl seats that recline. Instead, I squeeze myself onto wooden-slot benches in the second-class section.

It is New Delhi in June. The air is sweltering, but I choose the non-air-conditioned car. I am twenty-three years old, toward the end of a year traveling in Kenya and India. For a year I have carried all my possessions in my backpack, and I consider myself tough. From that train I take a bus and finally a cab. Jaiharikhal, my final destination, is a remote village high in the Himalayan mountains.

After beginning my day in the jostling sauna of New Delhi, I breathe a sigh of relief as the heat subsides and the crowds dwindle with each leg of the journey. By the time I arrive at my destination, the air is crisp and cool, the mountains are stunning, and there is not a soul to be seen. I struggle my pack onto my back and wander into the collection of flat-roofed buildings where I will spend the next few weeks. Finally a young Indian woman in a simple white sari finds me and, without speaking, brings me into what I later learn is the office. There is no desk and no chairs, just some papers strewn on a low table and four cushions scattered on the floor.

On one of the pillows, sitting in a lotus position with her back as straight as a ruler, is a woman with curly salt-and-pepper hair, dressed in a saffron robe. I recognize her outfit as the uniform of a *sannyasi*—someone, usually Hindu, who has renounced all worldly possessions, including family, profession, and home, in order to seek spiritual union. In this case, I know the saffron robe means something slightly different, for Vandana is a Sister of the Sacred Heart of Jesus, a member of a Christian order of religious women who are usually teachers.

Sister Vandana grew up Zoroastrian in Bombay, converted to Christianity as a young woman and joined the Sisters. After years as a teacher, she was drawn to a new movement in the Indian Catholic Church that seeks to engage in dialog with Hinduism. Unlike scholarly efforts to address theological parallels and contrasts, this movement explores ways Christians and Hindus can deepen their experiences of their own faith by learning from each other's ancient traditions and spiritual practices.

Sister Vandana is a leading voice in this new movement, and this collection of simple buildings in a remote village is the Jeevan Dhara ashram, one of a handful of communities dedicated to exploring the connection between Christian and Hindu spiritual practices.

In the five months I have been in India, I have visited at least a dozen ashrams, exploring the ways Indian women experience empowerment and fulfillment through their religious practices. In my letters back home, I describe an ashram as "sort of a cross between a monastery and a retreat center." Each ashram has *sannyasis* associated with it, people who have left their homes and professions to live permanently in a spiritual community. In addition, there are seekers who come to spend a week or a month on retreat to focus on their spiritual lives.

Almost always, the ashrams revolve around a guru, a spiritual leader who is more than just a teacher or guide. For many seekers, devotion to the guru is the pathway to God. Through the guru's compassion, they experience God's love. By following the guru's instructions, they grow spiritually. To my independent Western mind, it is a tough concept to embrace.

Some of the ashrams I visited confirmed my deeply ingrained suspicions. The gurus seemed like charlatans, abusing their power to gain wealth and devotion. Most of the gurus, though, emanated compassion and wisdom. I would sit for hours in the early morning chanting with hundreds of devotees and feel spiritual power rising in me. I'd have long conversations with women and men who found meaning and hope and healing through their devotion to their guru. I learned some hatha yoga postures, and I tried to sit still through long meditation sessions. Everywhere I went, I wrote assiduously in my journal, recording the stories people told me.

The trip to this ashram is different. This trip is not research. It is for me. I grew up Christian, active as a child and a youth in a church that encouraged us to think for ourselves and care for our neighbors. Midway through my freshman year in college, I had a flash of what seemed like a crazy idea—maybe I would become a minister. The flash came during a time I was questioning every aspect of my inherited faith, and it set in motion even deeper questioning.

Throughout college I took lots of religion courses—the best way I knew to get at my questions. I read critique after critique of Christianity, and I did some exploring of alternatives. In a semester abroad, and then during this year of independent study and travel, I focused on other people's spiritual lives—again, the best I could do at the time as I tried to figure out my own spiritual yearnings and path. When I learned about these Christian ashrams, I knew this was the next phase in my journey.

So now I kneel down in front of Sister Vandana and bow, a gesture of respect to the guru of this ashram. Without ceremony, she tells me this is the last conversation she will have with me for the next three days.

"The ashram has been a very busy place," she explains. "We had a very large group come for a retreat. Now we need our own retreat time." She goes on, "For the next three days, we will be in complete silence. After that, every morning will be silent, and all day every Friday will be silent."

I have lots of questions. Three days of silence? Why didn't you tell me this when I wrote to ask if I could come? How will I know what to do? Who's going to guide my meditation time? I don't ask any of them.

Sister Vandana calls the young girl in the white sari to show me to my room.

Like most of the ashram rooms where I've stayed,

this one is stark: a concrete square in a concrete block building, a cot for a bed, a table and chair and a yoga mat in the corner. What sets this room apart is the view out the solitary window: jagged, snow-covered peaks, occasionally crisp and clear, often obscured by clouds.

Once I settle in, those three days feel like a deep breath. I take long walks along the winding roads around the village, relieved not to be lugging my oversized backpack. I fall asleep reading in the afternoons; I didn't realize how worn out I was. I watch the five other ashram residents and figure out the signals for passing the tea and lentils during silent meals. The only speaking is during worship—morning and evening prayers, mass at noon. I quickly figure out that the one male at the ashram is a Catholic priest. He leads mass seated on a cushion on the floor, part of our circle. The worship is simple: scripture, prayers, a haunting Sanskrit chant—*"Jeevan ki roti mai hun."* It isn't until we can finally talk that I learn the words come from the gospel according to John: "I am the bread of life." There is no Catholic-Protestant anxiety about who can receive communion; the bread and cup are passed on a tray from person to person. By the time the three days of silence are over, I am settling into a routine with these five people whose names I barely know.

Still, I am relieved when we can finally talk to each other—at least during non-Friday afternoons. Now I can ask my questions, figure out who these people are and why they are here, and maybe even begin to figure that out for myself.

Sister Vandana is the center of ashram life. We call her Vandana-mataji—Mother Vandana—a title of deep respect. Tall, stately, almost regal, she is a powerful presence. I can imagine her as the school principal she once was. Always charismatic, occasionally imperious, she has a vision for this ashram and for the unique role of Indian Christianity. One day I ask her about her role. "I've been to a lot of Hindu ashrams," I begin, "and I am starting to get what the guru does there. But what about in a Christian ashram? Is it the same?"

At first I think I have offended her. "I am the guru here. I am the teacher. I am the leader and the guide of this ashram." Her tone softens, and I realize she is not offended. "Here it is different. Here I am the guru, but Jesus is the sat-guru—the head guru. My job," she goes on, "is to point to the sat-guru."

Wherever Vandana-mataji is found, so too can I find the two young Indian women dressed in plain white saris. Amita and Suli are novices in the Society of the Sacred Heart of Jesus. To them, Vandana-mataji is not only guru but also mistress of the novices. She guides them through their first year of religious life, sometimes gently, sometimes playfully, sometimes like a dictator.

There is also a woman from Germany at the ashram. Like many of the young Europeans I meet this year, Ursula is spending a few years seeing the world, searching for something. She grew up in a secular family, with no religious training. By the time I arrive, she has already been at the ashram for several months. She has never been baptized, and one afternoon I overhear Vandana-mataji and the priest debating whether it is okay to give her communion. At first, they put a flower on the communion tray for her to receive instead of the elements. A few days after that conversation, the flower disappears, and Ursula begins eating the bread and sipping from the cup.

Father Josep, the Catholic priest, is originally from Austria, but he has served for many years as a priest in South Africa. Before that, he traveled the world. When he was in Japan, he studied Buddhism and discovered Zen meditation. He went back to South Africa passionate about this spiritual practice. When he tried to teach his parishioners to meditate using Zen techniques, though, he had little success. Slowly, as he came to value what he called the "deeply expressive spirits" of his South African congregants, he realized that Zen was not the right approach. So he came to India to study ancient Hindu practices—hatha yoga and meditation. He hoped the physical movement of the yoga asanas would allow room for expression.

When he is bitten by a scorpion one night, I begin to understand how seriously Seppji, as we call him, takes his meditation practice. I learn about the bite after evening prayers, and worry that night about whether he will be okay. The next morning he breaks the breakfast silence to tell us about his night. He sat for hours outside his room meditating. Sitting perfectly still, he felt the poison spread up his arm toward his shoulder, and then, slowly, he felt the healing power of his own body—or the healing power of the Spirit within him—push the poison back down. By morning, the swelling and the pain were gone. For Seppji, meditation is truly life-giving.

Throughout college, much of my exploration about religion—and especially about Christianity centered on the role of women, and on the impact masculine and feminine images of the divine have on how we understand ourselves. I am intrigued and pleased that Jeevan Dhara has a female guru, and I am irritated that even this charismatic, groundbreaking guru needs a male priest to consecrate communion. So I am surprised, and a little disappointed, that Seppji is the one who becomes my mentor. When the three days of silence are over, Seppji announces that he will be resuming his daily routine on the flat roof of the dormitory, and we are invited to join him. The routine begins at 4:00 a.m., with an hour of hatha yoga followed by an hour of silent meditation, all before breakfast. Seppji climbs back onto the roof at 4:00 in the afternoon, for another two-hour stint.

Eager for structure and connection, I set my alarm clock for 3:45 and join him. Sometimes Ursula comes as well. Seppji is a patient and persistent teacher. I learned some yoga during my sojourns to other ashrams, and I sat in many an ashram hall for hours of meditation. I'm not a complete beginner. But this individual attention is different.

My favorite moment of the morning practice comes toward the end of the hour of yoga postures, when we stand in *vrikshasana,* the tree pose, balancing on one leg with our arms extended upward, hands clasped in a gesture of prayer. We face east just as the sky begins to lighten over the mountains. It takes me a week to get my balance, but once I find it, I feel as though I can stand there forever, my body honoring the beauty emerging into view. After tree pose, we lie down into *shavasana,* corpse pose, before sitting up for our hour of meditation.

As the days wear on, I feel something shift

inside me. I was an athlete in college, but this consistent, in-depth practice of hatha yoga is an entirely new experience of my body. The change is partly physical: my muscles have always been stiff, but in these weeks my body becomes as flexible as a gymnast's. I can bend over with straight knees and rest my palms on the ground; I can sit with my legs outstretched and rest my torso on my knees. More importantly, I begin to notice my body, to be present to the stretch of my muscles in a posture, to breathe and feel my breath moving through every part of me. Somewhere in those long hours of practicing being present to my body, I realize how much of my life I spend in my head, as though my body were just there to hold it in place.

As wonderful as the hatha yoga is, the time of simply sitting is even more powerful. I struggle with a mind that leaps and races and twists itself around in all sorts of contortions. Perhaps the greatest gift Seppji gives me is permission to stop trying to beat my mind into submission.

One evening after our meditation time, I sit with him on the concrete stoop outside his room. He had invited me to come by to talk about what I have been experiencing. I am frustrated. "I can't get my mind to be still," I complain. "And it's getting worse; out of nowhere I'll suddenly have this memory of something that happened ten years ago."

A grin breaks out on Seppji's face. "That's what happens," he says almost gleefully. "It's like therapy. All the old memories come up. It's like telling them to a therapist and then they stop having so much power in your life." Seppji is excited. "The difference," he continues, "is that God is the therapist. You don't have to do anything, just let those memories float in and float away and let God do the work."

And so I do. I stop worrying about slowing down my mind, and I begin to trust that whatever is happening in that hour of meditation is what needs to happen. I have a sense of freedom—from things that have trapped me my entire life: judgments I make about myself, changes I despair of ever making. More than anything else, what I experience in those long hours on the roof is permission to stop fighting so hard. Once I stop fighting, I feel knots begin to loosen.

One of those knots is my relationship with God. As I sit on that rooftop, I begin to let go of the sense that I am searching for God, even chasing after an elusive God who refuses to be "caught." Instead, I allow myself to trust that God is not playing hide-and-seek with me. God is already with me, waiting for me to notice, waiting for me to receive the gifts God holds out. As I sit, I feel myself opening to God's presence, accepting those gifts with gratitude.

With Seppji's gentle guidance, in a setting of stunning beauty, and in the context of a rigorous spiritual practice, I feel God's healing love change me. I learn that Jeevan Dhara is Sanskrit for "living water," and in my weeks there, I experience that living, healing, restoring water flow over and through me.

Part of the gift of Seppji's rigorous yoga and meditation practice, ironically, is that it allows me to be in control of letting go of control. It is my choice to get up at 3:45 in the morning. It is my choice to sit still for hours on end. My part in my own healing is to show up, and then I can, at least in theory, let God do the work.

Ursula occasionally sleeps in, but I am up on the roof every morning at 4:00. Even Seppji take Friday mornings off, but I don't. I am determined to do everything I can to allow myself to be less determined. I am working hard at letting go.

One morning I finally awaken to the irony of my determination. As always, I meet Seppji on the roof and we begin our routine. As always, he speaks only to guide us through the *asanas* and move us into the meditation time. When the two hours are over, he and I nod to each other with the namaste gesture of respect, and head to our rooms to get ready for breakfast. By the time we join the others for our normally silent breakfast, Seppji can no longer maintain the routine.

"Did you see it?" he asks eagerly. "Did you see it?"

"See what?" I am perplexed.

He looks shocked. "The mountains! Just after the sun rose, the clouds parted and you could see the mountain peaks. I've never seen them so clearly before. You didn't see it?" He is incredulous. "How could you miss it?"

"My eyes were closed," I answer. "I was meditating."

"Right. Of course." He looks disappointed.

"How did you see it?" I ask.

"This morning," he replies, "it was so beautiful I meditated with my eyes open."

"Oh." I am still confused. "I didn't know you could do that."

Slowly I begin to get it. The technique that opens me to God's love kept me from noticing God's beauty. The technique matters. The discipline of the practice matters—but only to a point.

I stay at Jeevan Dhara ashram for three weeks—a week more than I originally planned. Then, with great reluctance and a shock to my system, I get back into the taxi, onto the bus and then the train, back to the sweltering heat of New Delhi, soon to board an airplane to Kenya and eventually home.

I hear the sound of someone clearing his throat, and I open my eyes to see a porter in a neatly pressed blue uniform standing over me. He says something I don't understand. The young man in the seat beside me translates.

"Do you want chicken or lentils for lunch?"

Still back in Jaiharikhal, in my twenty-three-year-old self, I ask reflexively, "How much does it cost?"

"Oh, it's included in the price of the ticket," the young man replies. The trains have changed a lot. I choose the lentils, in honor of the many meals of lentils I ate in the old Jeevan Dhara ashram, in expectation of the meals I will have at the new ashram.

A lot has happened in the twenty-two years between that experience at the Jeevan Dhara ashram in Jaiharikhal and this return trip to India. I went to Divinity School and decided there really was something behind that flash I came to name as a call to ministry. I was ordained, met my partner Fran, and slowly lived into the role of pastor. I reveled in the miracle that I could come up with something to say almost every single Sunday, and that sometimes what I said awakened a new possibility for a member of the congregation. I discovered the depths of my capacity for compassion. Throughout those years, in varying degrees, the meditation practice I began at Jeevan Dhara remained an important part of my life.

When I first got home, and into my first few years in Divinity School, I was assiduous about my practice, with the same determination that led me to miss the sunlight on the Himalayan peaks. As my schedule grew more demanding, my determination softened—sometimes into a blessed flexibility, other times into an absence of consistency. There was a period of almost five years when I didn't meditate at all. Ultimately I rediscovered the power of simply sitting still.

Through all those years, I held on to the memory of the Jeeven Dhara ashram, hoping someday I could return. So when it came time for my second sabbatical, I began to dream. I searched the internet for signs of the ashram's continued existence. The best I could do was to order an out-of-print book Sister Vandana had written in the 1980's. When it arrived, as I had hoped, there was contact information on the back cover. It listed two addresses: the ashram I remembered in Jaiharikhal and another one in Rishikesh, a holy city north of Delhi, along the Ganges River, which was known as the "yoga capital of the world." Feeling quite old-fashioned but with no other choice, I sat down and wrote two identical letters to Vandana-mataji, telling her how much my 1985 stay at Jeevan Dhara had changed my life, and asking whether I could come again.

Three weeks later an email popped up in my AOL account. It was from Sister Tureeya, the new spiritual leader of the Jeevan Dhara Ashram. She had received my letter in Rishikesh and kindly explained that Vandana-mataji was in the mid-stages of Alzheimer's Disease and had moved to an ashram in Southern India, where other sisters were caring for her. She also told me that the ashram in Jaiharikhal had been sold. I was most welcome, she wrote, to come stay at the ashram in Rishikesh.

I was excited and disappointed. I was prepared to get no response at all, to be forced to conclude that the ashram was long gone. So I was thrilled to hear from Sister Tureeya, but sad to face the reality that this would be a different trip to a different ashram with a different guru.

"A different trip to a different ashram with a different guru," I mutter to myself over and over again as I pull myself back into the present. "Don't expect this to be like last time," I warn myself. "It's not up in the mountains. Sister Vandana won't be there—and neither will Father Seppji." I remind myself that I have changed also. As hard as I work to manage my expectations, I am primed for peace and beauty, for a wise mentor and a life-changing experience.

As we approach Haridwar, the destination of the train, I strike up a conversation with my seat mate, a young, casually-dressed man named Krishna who has spent the trip running up and down the aisle and talking on his cell phone. I ask him where he is going.

"To Rishikesh."

"Me too." I answer. "Have you heard of an ashram called Jeevan Dhara?"

"No…but I don't know a lot about the ashrams there."

"What are you going to do in Rishikesh?"

"Rafting on the Ganges River."

"Really?" I wonder how a man with a name like Krishna can go rafting on the holy Hindu river.

Krishna is happy to explain. "I work for a tour company. We do team building events for businesses in New Delhi. Today I'm taking a bunch of software engineers—we're going rafting."

"On the Ganges River?"

"Yeah, it's the best. Really wild. And then there's the leaping rock. We'll raft down the river to the rock, and then we'll see who's got the guts to jump off."

"Have you jumped off?" I ask.

"Every time." Then he leaps up and heads down the aisle one more time, checking to make sure his software engineers are all happy and ready for their trip to the holy city of Rishikesh. They are not pilgrims, seeking to bathe in the holy river that has been the destination for millennia. They are adventure-seekers, eagerly debating who will have the courage to jump off the famous leaping rock into the river.

Krishna comes back to his seat. In my perpetual effort not to be cheated, I ask him how much I should pay for a taxi to Rishikesh, and how long it should take.

"No more than 100 rupees," he says, "and no more than an hour."

The train stops. I wrestle my bag down from the overhead compartment and step out into the city of Haridwar. Like Rishikesh, and every other place along the Ganges River, Haridwar is considered a holy city, with ashrams and seekers, teachers and charlatans.

A young man approaches me. "Where are you going?"

"Rishikesh—Jeevan Dhara ashram." I am sure he will know it.

He doesn't. But he is not deterred. "Rishikesh—

come, I will take you to Rishikesh."

"How much?"—my favorite question.

"Eighty rupees."

A bargain, I think to myself.

He grabs my bag and I follow him—past rows and rows of old black taxis. We walk until we stop beside a battered auto-rickshaw. "You're going to take me all the way to Rishikesh in this?"

"Sure, sure, no problem." I get in.

We putt and bump along the dirty, stone-filled road. The dust flies into my face every time a taxi whips by. Oh well, I think, at least I am saving 20 rupees.

I begin to worry when he stops at a deserted field alongside the river. "What are you doing?" I ask.

"I can't take you any further. Not allowed to go to Rishikesh."

I am livid. "What? You told me...."

Just then another, even more battered, auto-rickshaw drives up. My driver leaps out of his vehicle, grabs my bag, puts it in the other rickshaw, and beckons for me to come. "Still 80 rupees," I demand—as though I have any choice.

"Sure, sure, no problem."

I show my new chauffeur the printed email with

directions to the Jeevan Dhara ashram. It makes no sense to him, but we set off anyway. We putt our way along more dirt roads until we approach the city. It's not an impressive approach. An old tire warehouse and junkyard offer the first hints we are getting close, then a video store, and finally internet cafes, hotels, souvenir shops, and people. There are lots of people, clearly from all over the world. A holy tourist town.

The driver tries to dump me out in the center of town. "No," I say firmly, "you have to take me to the ashram."

He grows more and more nervous. "But madam, I am not allowed to go any further. No auto-rickshaws allowed here." He gets out several times to try to find someone who has heard of the ashram.

Finally, he stops at the end of a road. There is no ashram in sight, just a long concrete path, wider than a sidewalk but too narrow for a road. "Down there," he points. I ask if he will carry my bag for an extra 50 rupees, but he just wants to get out of town.

I put my bag over my shoulder and start to walk. I've only taken a few steps when I notice the cow in the center of the path. I'm neither surprised nor concerned. Cows are everywhere in India; considered holy and never eaten, they are treated with respect and allowed to roam at will. I've walked past many cows on this trip, and even more on my last visit.

This cow is different. She comes right up to me and gores me with her horns. Looking calm and peaceful, she rams one horn into my side while the other catches my wrist. Then she turns and walks away.

I walk away, too, as quickly as my overflowing duffle bag will let me. I am stunned. I look back over my shoulder. The irate cow is long gone. My ribs hurt, and my arm is stinging. I keep walking; I don't know what else to do. A few blocks down the path, I see a faint sign on a blue steel door: "Jeeven Dhara," it says. I have arrived.

The door is padlocked. I bang on the steel, then peer over the stone wall into a tiny compound, but there is no one in sight.

As I sit down on my duffle bag to consider my next move, I notice my watch is not on my wrist. I stand up and it falls out of my *kurta* sleeve. Apparently, the cow gored my watch and broke the band. The watch still tells time; I just can't get it to stay on my wrist.

I sit contemplating what this all might mean. A sacred cow gores me and breaks my watch. I wait at the entrance to Jeevan Dhara—the Living Water—but the gate is locked.

❊

✴ Later on Monday ✴
"Opening"

I wait outside the locked gate of the Living Waters, wondering what I will do if no one comes, pulling my broken watch out of my pocket every few moments to check the time. After a half hour, I see three people walk up the path. The woman, I assume, is Sister Tureeya. She is dressed in a saffron robe, like the Vandana-mataji of my memories. I guess she is about my age—mid-40's—with close cropped dark hair peeking out beneath her saffron scarf. Accompanying her is a younger man with sharp features and a shaved head, wearing a plain grey t-shirt and loose drawstring pants. He is carrying a large propane tank on his right shoulder. The third in the trio is a disheveled elderly man with an uncombed shock of grey hair over a deeply wrinkled face. He wears a dirty white t-shirt and a blue and grey striped cloth pulled up between his legs in the traditional Indian fashion.

I stand up as they approach.

"We thought you would be here hours ago." That is Sister Tureeya's idea of a greeting.

"I would have been, but I made the mistake of taking an auto-rickshaw instead of a taxi, and then the driver had to stop…"

The good sister cuts me off. "You have to be careful with those drivers," she warns me. Then she unlocks the blue steel door.

The compound is immaculate and sparse. Concrete sidewalks are broken up by squares and rectangles of shrubs and small trees. There are several white concrete block buildings, not unlike the Jeevan Dhara of my memory, but crammed together and without benefit of mountain scenery.

Sister Tureeya snaps at the old man, saying something in Hindi I can only interpret as an order given to a servant. She nods curtly to the young man as he puts the propane tank down beside the kitchen. Then she smiles at me and takes me to my room.

It is exactly what I have come to expect with ashrams: a concrete floor, bare concrete-block walls, a cot-like bed, a TV tray for a table, and a metal folding chair. Everything is grey. The one luxury item is a ceiling fan, which I am already grateful to have.

Sister Tureeya shows me a card. "Here's the schedule for the ashram. Morning meditation is at

4:30 a.m., with breakfast at 7:00. We meditate at 11:00 a.m. followed by lunch at 12:30 p.m. Afternoon meditation is at 3:00, tea at 4:15. We end the day with 6:00 p.m. meditation and dinner at 7:30." Meditate and eat—that appears to be the order of the day.

"Do you do any yoga?" I ask hopefully.

"Not here. Juan goes to classes in town, but you should not do that. You can do yoga in your room if you must. Our focus here is on the contemplative life."

"Today we missed our afternoon meditation," Sister Tureeya goes on. "We had to take the old man to the doctor. That strange cow gored him earlier today."

I interrupt to tell my cow-goring story. "That happened to me too; in fact the cow broke my watch…"

She interrupts me back. "Now I need to go fix tea. Come in 15 minutes." And she leaves me to unpack.

Tea time is held in a screened-in room. There is one stool and one tray, and a collection of pillows and placemats on the floor. The stool and tray, I learn, are for the old man. He smiles at me when I greet him—"Namaste," the only word I remember from my futile attempt to learn the language on my first trip. He brings his hands into the prayer position that is the classic greeting and responds, "Namaste." That is the extent of our cross-cultural conversation. Sister Tureeya is alternately snippy and solicitous with him, making sure he gets his tea exactly the way he likes it, then shaking her head in disgust at him, as she mutters, "lazy, lazy, lazy" under her breath. I conclude that he is an employee—part gardener, part vegetable-chopper.

The young, sharp-featured man is sitting in his place on the floor, having pushed his pillow out of the way. His back is ram-rod straight. Since it appears no one is going to introduce me formally, I look over at him and greet him, "Namaste. My name is Debbie."

He replies in kind, "Namaste. I am Juan." His English is excellent; his accent is strong. That seems to be the end of the conversation, but I persist.

"Where are you from?"

"Spain." His voice is so quiet I have to lean in to hear him.

"How long have you been here?"

"Three months, but before I was at another ashram."

"What brings you to India?"

"Yoga and meditation. I meditate here, but I go

for advanced yoga classes in town."

"How long will you stay in India?"

"I will stay until my visa runs out. That's what I have been doing for the last three years."

The more questions I ask, the shorter and quieter his answers become. Finally we happen upon the one topic that brings him to life. His voice grows strong and steady as he tells me about his study of *pranayama*, yogic breathing techniques. I can hear his passion and his pride. "I have been trying for months, and last week, finally, I learned how to make the *aum* sound vibrate in all the different parts of my body."

As the four of us sit in that screened-in dining area, I can feel the tension. Sister Tureeya is kind to me, if a bit short, but there is little kindness in the clipped way she speaks to Juan. She is clearly not impressed by his *aum* vibration achievement. "You are making yoga too important," she tells him. She seems to care about him, though she shows it in an odd way: "Here, eat these cookies. You are too skinny." Her frustration at him comes through in her housekeeping comments: "I told you many times not to wash your clothes in the middle of the day, when the water's scarce. Why won't you listen to me?"

Juan's responses are alternately sullen and irritated: "Yes mataji," as though she is his mother and he a recalcitrant teenager. "My clothes were dirty; I had to wash them." "The swamis say *pranayama* is the gateway to enlightenment."

The elderly man sits on his stool oblivious to the English conversation, periodically pointing at the thermos of tea or the plate of store-bought cookies.

The tension breaks when a young woman knocks on the screen door. Sister Tureeya leaps up to greet her with a broad smile and invites her in for tea. She is so glad to see this young woman that she actually introduces her to me. "Maria, this is Debbie. She just came from America. Debbie, this is Maria. She is from Spain."

I no longer have to pull teeth to keep the conversation pleasant. "Maria," Sister Tureeya begins, "is here on her fourth trip to India."

"What brings you to India?" I ask the same question I asked Juan, but with a much more satisfying response.

"I was searching for something, and I found it in India. It is my spiritual home." She pauses for a moment. "This trip, though, I am not so sure. Something feels different, but I don't know what."

"Are you staying here at Jeevan Dhara?" I ask, hopefully. When she is here Sister Tureeya is different.

"No, I'm staying at another ashram in Rishikesh." Smart woman, I think to myself. "I like to come here, though, especially for tea and to talk with the Sister."

Maria and Sister Tureeya start in on their own conversation—about a festival in town and the church down the road. As they speak, I catch a glimpse of the sister's passion for what she understands to be her purpose: to build relationships and connections among spiritual seekers from different traditions. Both Maria and Juan come from Catholic backgrounds, and both are seeking spiritual nourishment through Hindu practices. With Maria, it seems, Sister Tureeya is able to help bring the past and the present—Christian background and Hindu practices—together. With Juan, she seems to have given up.

Relieved, I breathe in the more relaxed atmosphere Maria's presence brings. The next knock on the door, though, restores the tension on the porch and lifts it to an even higher level. A tall blond man with a slightly receding hairline walks in.

"So what is it you want anyway?" Sister Tureeya snaps at him. "Sit down and have tea." Her tone belies the offer of hospitality.

"Hello, my name is Chretien—Christian in English." He is the first person to take the initiative to introduce himself to me. He sits down on the one empty pillow, which happens to be beside me. Sister Tureeya shoves the thermos in his direction and goes to get another cup and saucer. Once again, I try to ease the tension by making small talk.

"Are you staying here at Jeevan Dhara?" I ask.

"Only for tonight, I guess." Like Juan and Maria and Sister Tureeya, Chretien speaks excellent English with a strong accent; his accent is French. "I left my backpack here earlier today and went to see about another place I'd heard of—but they won't have a room until tomorrow. So I'll stay here tonight, though the sister doesn't seem to like me much."

I don't know how to respond. I am taken aback by the harshness of Sister Tureeya's treatment of Chretien—but I am also taken aback by Chretien's use of this ashram as a cheap hotel. He is not here to engage in Christian-Hindu dialog. The rules of ashram hospitality apparently do not allow Sister Tureeya to tell him no, but they don't stop her from being rude to him.

This odd mix of tension and compassion, hospitality and harshness, continues through the evening meditation and dinner. As I force myself to try to sleep at 8:30 p.m., I wonder whether the sacred cow was warning me that the living waters here have gone stagnant. Maybe, I think, it would have been better if the gate had remained closed.

⁕

✳ Tuesday ✳
"The Spirit Sputters and Soars"

My travel alarm sets off its pathetic but startling beep at 4:10 in the morning. I leap out of my cot onto the cold concrete floor. I move quickly. I have a strong sense it is not good to be late for meditation at this ashram.

I climb the outdoor stairs and step into the chapel, seven minutes early. Sister Tureeya and Juan are sitting in lotus position, already deep in meditation. I pull my broken watch out of my pocket and check it against the clock ticking away on the wall. No, I am not late. My watch's encounter with the sacred cow did not break the mechanism.

I sit down on a small pile of pillows and try to adjust them so my back will be straight and my knees supported. I take a few deep breaths and wait for the clock to turn to 4:30. Surely Sister Tureeya, as spiritual leader of the ashram, will say something to lead us into meditation as a community. 4:30 comes and goes and she doesn't move. At 4:35 Chretien comes in and sits down. This time Tureeya opens her eyes, but just long enough to glare at him. I was right that I do not want to be late to meditation.

After Sister Tureeya's glaring look at Chretien, I conclude there will not be an official start to the morning meditation. I close my eyes and begin to repeat my mantra.

"Open," I whisper to myself as I breathe out. I straighten my back. I readjust my ankles in my half-lotus position (no way I will ever get into Juan and Sister Tureeya's full lotus), trying to get them so they will not dig into my thighs. I breathe in and then out again. "Open." I try to ignore the clock ticking loudly on the wall, and then I tell myself not to worry about ignoring it. "Open…"

Usually, I love to meditate with other people. I love the sense that the peace one of us breathes out is peace another one can breathe in. I love the feeling that my meditation is not just for myself, but for the people sitting beside me, whose needs and language I may not know and don't need to know. And I love that their meditation is also for me.

Today it feels different. We aren't meditating together, just in the same room. The energy they breathe out is the energy I breathe in. It doesn't feel like healing energy, though, not the peace that comes from sitting in the presence of the sacred. It is—or so it feels to me—the energy of frustration. It is, I imagine, the energy of meditation that is striving rather than letting go.

Meditation, according to the schedule Sister Tureeya gave me yesterday, is supposed to last an hour, but at 5:15 I open my eyes when I hear Juan unfold his body, get up, and leave. He has to get to his yoga class in town. Soon thereafter, Sister Tureeya rustles around, gets up and walks out, not quite slamming the door but almost.

Chretien and I stay. I focus on my breath, trying to breathe peace into this tense room, into this strange ashram. I'm not sure I can.

When I peek again at the clock, it says 5:30. Chretien and I get up and head back to our rooms.

Sister Tureeya intercepts me before I make it to my concrete block. "Come," she says curtly, "you can help." We go into the kitchen, a small, dark room with pots and pans hanging on the wall, a sink and a wooden counter, and an old-fashioned propane stove. She hands me a bowl of *chapatti* dough. "Here, make this into balls." She rolls one, the size of a golf-ball, as an example. "Be sure they are all the same size, or they won't cook evenly."

We form a mini-assembly line. I roll the dough into balls with my hands, and she takes out her rolling pin, flattens them into perfect circles and puts them onto the dry frying pan to cook. When I hand her one that is just the right size, she nods with satisfaction. When I don't get it quite right, she returns them to me: "too big," "too small," "make this one rounder."

I try to start conversation—"I'm so glad to learn how to do this. On my last trip the family I stayed with in Delhi tried to teach me, but I never…"

She cuts me off. "Do this one over." Sister Tureeya is reaching out to me, but on her own terms.

Even with my periodic do-overs, I eventually get ahead of her, so she lets me take a turn cooking them—an even more exacting job, I quickly learn. If you turn them too soon, they lose their shape. If you turn them too late, they burn. And then, once they are done in the frying pan, you have to put them directly on the stove for just a few seconds so they can puff up and crisp. I never master that part, but she does let me try.

In another place and time, that kitchen would be filled with gentle laughter at my awkward attempts at cross-cultural cooking. Here there is no laughter, but also no tension. Just two people working in the kitchen. When we are done, she dismisses me a few minutes before breakfast.

Unlike the Jeevan Dhara of my memories, this ashram does not have an intentionally silent breakfast. Still, breakfast is silent. Chretien is there and seems afraid to speak. Sister Tureeya makes it very clear he is not welcome.

When the dishes are done, Sister Tureeya calls me over and whispers that she wants to show me some spiritual places this morning. We walk a few blocks into town and meet Maria in front of the only Christian church in Rishikesh. I would never have known it is a church: no cross, no sign, no steeple, just a compound wall with another one of those ubiquitous steel doors. We go in long enough for her to introduce me to the two priests—an older clean shaven man, and a young man with a beard.

"This is Reverend Debbie. She is a Christian minister from America." I hear the pride in her voice that a minister, a woman at that, is at her ashram.

"Namaste," they greet me. The priests are polite but not overly impressed. We go to wait for the bus.

At the bus stop, Maria asks me about my work. "I've never met a woman pastor before." Maria is the one person who seems to want to hear about my life, and I am happy to oblige.

I plunge into my standard description of my work and my church. "I preach every Sunday, except occasionally when my student gets a turn. Of course I go to lots of meetings and I teach Bible Study. I do lots of visiting of the people in the church, listening and praying and…"

Once again, Sister Tureeya interrupts. "Shhh!" Her whisper has an edge to it. "You're talking too loud." I am perplexed; I have never been accused of having a loud voice. "Don't talk about church things in public." She continues her critique: "And button the top button on your blouse." I have also never been accused of dressing in a provocative fashion. But I lower my voice, change the topic, and button my top button.

We hop onto a rickety bus. I forget all about the strange morning meditation and the awkward breakfast and my buttoned-to-the-neck shirt as the vehicle whips around corners and climbs higher and higher. It is a full-size bus overflowing with people; the road is narrow and there is no guard rail to protect us from the precipitous edge. The turns are hairpin. The trapped energy of unspoken anger, hushed conversation and buttoned-to-the-top blouses breaks free. There is an odd and terrifying joy in the chaotic, overflowing, overwhelming aliveness of the bus. I forget all about breathing out peace; it is all I can do to remember to breathe.

An hour later, Sister Tureeya pulls the cord and beckons to us to be ready. We get off at what seems to be just another curve in the road. But she knows where she is going. She leads us along a narrow path to a set of steep, crooked concrete stairs. We descend, find another set of stairs, and descend some more. Finally we reach a series of plain cement-block buildings. A bearded man in a saffron robe is hanging out his wash. He nods a greeting as we walk on to a shrine built into a hill.

Above the door is something written in Sanskrit. "The old swami who discovered this cave was a very wise man," Tureeya begins. "Those are his words. They are more beautiful in Sanskrit," she apologizes, and then she struggles to translate. "'We search everywhere outside for what we can only find within.' He discovered this cave fifty years ago but he could see it had been used by swamis for centuries before."

With those words of inspiration, we walk through the door and enter a small but deep cave. Tureeya pulls out her flashlight and leads us, stooped over, all the way to the back. She takes three small squares of tattered cloth out of her bag and hands one to each of us. "Here. Sit on this. We will do our meditation right here." She sits down and lights a candle someone else has placed on the floor.

Without pillows to arrange and rearrange, I struggle to get comfortable. My back doesn't want to stay straight; my knees are touching the cold, damp floor. I breathe in the musty, dank air. I sit still, I breathe in and out, I repeat my mantra, and I never feel myself move to a deeper level.

It is not a powerful meditation time for me, but it is powerful to be there. A comment my partner Fran made earlier in our sabbatical travels comes back to me as I sit. We were visiting an ancient statue of Buddha in Sri Lanka. The statue was impressive in size, beauty, and design. "What a holy place," Fran exclaimed. "You can feel it—so many prayers have been prayed here."

That's what this cave is like. My own meditation feels distracted and shallow, but it almost doesn't matter. What matters is that we are in a place made holy by the prayers of centuries of seekers. Somehow, even if I don't feel it, I am breathing in their yearnings and their peace. Somehow, I hope, our hour of silence adds to the sacred energy of the place.

It is a holy place because of the centuries of prayers offered here, and it is a holy place because Sister Tureeya has brought us. In less than 24 hours at the ashram, I have felt her anger and disappointment and fear. Now, she is entrusting Maria and me with a glimpse of her yearning, her passion, her desire for deep peace.

We emerge from the damp darkness into the sunlight and wander down to the banks of the holy Ganges River. It is shallow in this area, and we step from stone to stone. Maria takes off her shoes and dips her feet into the water. Then she bends over, cups water in her hands, tosses it into the air, and prays a blessing on the sun and on herself. I do the same. Sister Tureeya watches.

We sit on the rocks for a few minutes. This time Sister Tureeya doesn't interrupt our attempts at conversation. "This is what I love about India," Maria begins. "Back home, it feels so empty."

I don't have to ask any questions; Maria is ready to talk. "When my mother got sick, the priest told us to pray. We prayed and prayed and prayed—and the cancer spread. He said it must be God's will. I tried to accept it. I really did. I asked the priest why God would want my mother to suffer, and he told me not to question God. 'It's a mystery.'" As she quotes him, bitterness creeps into her voice.

"After her funeral, I couldn't sit through church. I went every Sunday, and sometimes even during the week. But every time I had to leave before it was over. I couldn't make myself go up for Eucharist. At first I was mad. Then I just felt empty—like God wasn't there."

"How did you end up coming to India?"

"I was desperate. I tried everything. Finally I went to the meditation center in my town. They had a class for beginners. The first time we sat in silence I wept—loud. I was out of control. I almost ran out of the room, but something told me it was okay to stay.

"The teacher was so kind. She said no one in the

room minded; they all knew what it was like. So I went back. Some days I cried. Some days this wave of sadness would wash over me. Sometimes I felt a tiny bit of peace.

"The center had a library. I started borrowing the books. I couldn't get enough of them. There was one, written by a guru of one of the ashrams in Rishikesh. When I read it, I knew I had to come.

"It took me a year to save up enough money. I asked for a leave of absence from my job, but they said no. I quit and came to the ashram for two months. I thought I was in heaven. The guru—it was like he already knew me. When the whole group meditated together, I felt something—we were all connected to each other. I'd never felt that before—not ever, not once in my church back home."

Maria pauses for a moment. I think longingly of the old Jeevan Dhara ashram and Father Seppji. Sister Tureeya, who has been listening quietly, now speaks, more tenderly than I thought possible.

"That's where Maria and I met—at that ashram. I'd gone there to talk with the guru—he is my friend. In fact, he was one of the *sannyasis* who came to my renunciation ceremony. He gave me my robes."

Maria smiles. "I was there for the ceremony. I got to see it."

"You see, this is what Christianity needs." Sister

Tureeya can't resist the chance to make her point. "Renunciation. Meditation. Contemplation. We need to stop talking about God and start listening.... Come on. Let's go. We've got to go see an old swami."

We begin our ascent—up the two steep flights of stairs, back to the main road, around a corner, then up another hill and another set of hidden stairs. The stairs lead us to a tiny, rundown house with saffron-colored laundry hanging on a line. Sister Tureeya knocks. We wait. She knocks again. We sit down on the stoop and wait some more. "I think the old man might be getting deaf," she says. We wait longer. She knocks again. This time we hear footsteps and the door opens. A wizened old man stands in the doorway with his hands in prayer position—"Namaste." For the first time since I arrived at Jeevan Dhara, I feel the meaning behind the traditional blessing—"The sacred in me honors the sacred in you."

"Namaste," we reply.

If the twenty-minute wait is an indication of reluctance to welcome strangers into his isolated home, his greeting does not betray it. His arms open wide. "Come in, come in."

I am surprised to hear him speak English. As the conversation evolves, he moves back and forth between English and his native Hindi. Tureeya is a remarkably attentive translator, keeping Maria and me informed about the topic of conversation at all times.

Sister Tureeya inquires after his health. Swamiji, as she calls him, smiles broadly and lifts his arms to the sky. "I am ninety years old. I eat only fruit and vegetables. I am very healthy."

We soon get to the purpose of the visit. Sister Tureeya pulls a folder out of her bag. It contains the medical records of a sister from her order in Bombay. "This sister has been diagnosed with cancer. I am hoping you can give me a recommendation for her treatment."

Swamiji takes the file and studies it. "The whole problem," he says in English, "started when the sister had a hysterectomy. If she had addressed the original symptoms with homeopathy instead of surgery, none of this would have happened." He shakes his head with disdain.

"So what should she do?" Sister Tureeya asks, pen and paper in hand. Swamiji takes a deep breath.

"I cannot know without examining her in person," he replies. Tureeya looks disappointed, but he will not budge. Finally he digs through some papers on a table and gives her the name of a Zoroastrian healer he knows in Bombay.

Sister Tureeya seems to be getting ready to thank him and go, but Maria speaks up. "I have these really sweaty palms," she begins. "Is there something you can do to help them?"

Swamiji smiles, thrilled to be asked. "Anything else?" he asks.

"Well," she says, "I don't know if it's related, but I have this discoloration of the skin on my face."

Swamiji ponders. "Anything else?" he asks a second time.

"I don't think so," Maria replies.

But then Sister Tureeya jumps in. "What about your allergies?"

"That's right," Maria begins to put things together. "I am allergic to so many things—nuts, grass, dust, milk…"

Swamiji wonders aloud. "It might be your liver." But he wants confirmation. He tells Maria to lie down on the concrete floor while he gets out his pendulum—a magnet on a string. One by one, he touches each of her *chakras* with one hand while he holds up the pendulum with the other hand. "Is this *chakra* operating well?" he asks aloud, and then waits for the pendulum to begin its circle. Clockwise, clockwise, clockwise, until he gets to the liver *chakra*. The pendulum reverses its direction, slowly circling counter-clockwise.

"The problem is in your liver," he concludes, and he prescribes a very specific quantity and concentration of certain drops. "This medicine," he explains, "when given in the right, infinitesimal dose, will solve the problem. If it is given in a larger dose, it will cause the problem."

Swamiji goes on to explain the dilemma of dosage in the modern world. "Homeopathy," he tells us, "is an ancient practice. The proper dosages have been perfected over centuries. Now, though, the air is polluted and our food is very unhealthy." He gets that look of disdain again. "So the old dosages are no longer sufficient." He turns to Maria. "That is why other homeopaths have not been able to help you; most of them are using dosages appropriate for 300 years ago, but not for today."

All this time, I have been watching and listening. Now Swamiji turns to me. "What about you? Do you have any ailments?"

I wish I could come up with one. There is frustration with my meditation practice, disappointment with the ashram, homesickness…but nothing physical. It feels too forward to ask if he will read my *chakras* and see if he can find any problems. So I shake my head. "No, thank you though."

Sister Tureeya digs down in her bag and pulls

out her wallet, but Swamiji waves her away. "Oh no," he says, "I cannot take money; it would ruin the healing." Tureeya tries again, but he is adamant. He is a healer; he does not take money. "Next time we will bring you some fruit," Tureeya concludes. Swamiji smiles broadly. We thank him profusely and leave.

By now it is mid-morning, and the sun is beating down on us as we descend the hill and wait for the bus. The bus is packed, and the air in it is stifling. After we bid farewell to Maria in town, we go back to the ashram. The peaceful energy of the cave, the healing energy of Swamiji's home, the wild energy of the bus—they give way to the choked energy of an awkward and tense lunch back in the screened-in porch.

We are eating together, and this morning we prayed together, so I guess that makes us community. It certainly makes us connected with each other. But in that porch, our connections feel like entanglements. Juan's passion for his yoga class doesn't energize Tureeya's passion for her ministry; if anything, it yanks at it, tightening the knot of their entanglement. Tureeya's rudeness toward Chretien, well-deserved as it might be, leaves me distrustful of her kindness toward me.

Once or twice during lunch, the awkward silence

erupts into argument, as Tureeya bristles at a dismissive comment Juan makes about Christianity or scolds the old man for not chopping the vegetables right. I don't know where to look or what to say as the words swirl around. Still, I am relieved when they break through. At least the energy is visible, audible, swirling instead of stifling.

Back at the other Jeevan Dhara ashram, so many years ago, I read all the books by the gurus of the then-thriving Christian-Hindu ashram movement. Each of them had their own interpretation of the parallels between Hindu philosophy and Christian theology. Most of them drew a connection between the Hindu concept of *atman*—the human soul which is ultimately one with God—and the Holy Spirit. I found myself making a different set of parallels. I was intrigued by the Hindu concept of **Shakti**, which I understood to be the energy that animates us, the energy that swirls around us, the wild and sometimes chaotic movement of wind and breath, conversation and connection. *Shakti* is a goddess, a feminine energy moving through our world.

On that first trip, I began to see a parallel between *Shakti* and the Holy Spirit. While Vandanamataji and Father Seppji understood the Holy Spirit as a still, unmoving, unchanging place deep within us, I was drawn to the Spirit as movement, breath, action, energy. I still am.

It is the Holy Spirit—*Shakti*—making a tentative connection between Sister Tureeya and me as she teaches me how to make *chapattis*. It is the Holy Spirit careening around the corners and animating conversations on that bus. It is the Spirit holding the prayers of centuries of seekers in the cave, waiting for us to breathe them in and offer more. It is the Spirit filling Swamiji and his visitors with healing energy.

And in the new Jeevan Dhara meditation room and dining porch? Perhaps what I feel is the Holy Spirit struggling to break free from all the barriers, all the pain and disappointment, anger and misunderstanding that is blocking her.

✻ Wednesday ✻
"Three Hours and Eighteen Minutes"

Juan says, "If you are meditating and you sit completely still for three hours and eighteen minutes," you will achieve *Samadhi*, a state of perfect peace." Midway through a pleasant, if hot and dusty, walk along a winding road, Juan shares the secret to enlightenment.

By Wednesday, I am settling in to the rhythm, strained as it is, of life at the Jeevan Dhara ashram. I've figured out that, after the early morning meditation, I have enough time before breakfast to take a thick blanket up to the roof of the dormitory for a little yoga. The view is nothing like the other Jeevan Dhara—just a bunch of flat roofs with laundry hanging out to dry. There is no Father Seppji to guide me. Still I am determined to make the best of it.

At breakfast, I interrupt the awkward silence. "I think I'll take a walk this morning."

I see the look on Sister Tureeya's face, the familiar expression I've come to recognize as disapproval. "Be very careful," she warns. "Be sure to button your blouse all the way. Don't look anyone in the eye, especially men. And whatever you do, don't talk to anyone."

She does everything she can to convince me to stay in my concrete block room. "You know it's going to be very hot out there."

"I know," I answer, "that's why I was thinking I would go now, before the sun gets too strong."

"The road is very dusty; you'll get your clothes dirty."

I've got an answer for that one too. "I've got the clothes I wore on the train on Monday. They are already dusty; a little more won't hurt."

She tries again. "There are a lot of strange people who come to Rishikesh."

I force a smile and keep my voice light. "I'll be very careful and I won't go far."

When she realizes I am going no matter what, Sister Tureeya leaves for a moment and comes back with a long scarf. "Here. Put this on. Be sure to keep your head covered."

Off I go, along the narrow path that was previously guarded by the goring cow, down a long flight of crooked steps into the bustling center of town.

I pass bookstores, coffee shops, a guy with a chimpanzee doing tricks, and an apparent swami with a wild mass of hair selling something. I walk across a narrow bridge that says it is for pedestrians, and I learn quickly that motorcycles and monkeys are considered pedestrians. I set off on a road that follows the Ganges River, hoping I will soon get past the crowds to feel the peacefulness of the holy water.

The crowds do thin out, and I find myself walking on a winding road that roughly parallels the river. But peace eludes me. Every time a truck drives by, I pull my scarf tighter around my head and try to look as small and unobtrusive as I can. Even as I wonder what has made Sister Tureeya so frightened, I feel myself taking her fear into my body. I slink along for a while, too timid to appreciate any beauty I see. I cut my walk short and head back early, with plenty of time to sit in my concrete block before 11 a.m. meditation.

At lunch, Sister Tureeya asks about my walk. I lie. "It was nice."

Juan jumps in, uncharacteristically talkative. "You like to walk? I'll show you some very nice walks here. I like to walk for hours." As a man, of course, Juan is exempt from the ashram requirement of keeping one's head covered and looking away from others in fear. "I like to walk along the river. First you have to cross the bridge—the one with the monkeys and the motorcycles, but then it's very peaceful and beautiful."

Peaceful and beautiful, I think to myself, if you're not scared of your shadow.

Juan goes on, excited. "Want me to show you my favorite ashram?"

It is April in Rishikesh, and by afternoon the sun is strong, but I jump at the chance to walk without worrying that I am supposed to be afraid. We wash our dishes and set off down the same path, across the same scooter-laden bridge, and along the same road winding beside the river.

Over the past few days, I have begun to get a sense of my mysterious ashram-mate. Juan is a man of few words, and the words he does speak are sometimes confusing, sometimes provocative, sometimes outrageous, and occasionally insightful. Most of the outrageous statements, or so it seems to me, are intended to goad Sister Tureeya into an argument, usually about Christianity. "It's all about dogma," he periodically asserts, implying that the Hindu philosophies behind his yoga and meditation practice are not.

Sister Tureeya denies it. "No," she says in an angry tone, "it's all about grace."

His confusing and provocative statements are generally about his yoga and meditation practice.

Over dinner my first night, he described his frustration that his foot falls asleep if he tries to meditate more than eight hours a day. Not sure why anyone would want to meditate that long, I nonetheless made a suggestion I thought to be eminently practical: "Why don't you try a different position, like sitting on a chair?"

Juan looked shocked. "When I meditate," he said, "I can feel my subtle body. My crossed legs make a knot so I can focus my energy on my upper body." I had no idea what he was talking about, but I got the point: meditating in a chair will definitely not do.

Juan's most insightful statements are the rare personal ones. "I couldn't live in this world," he blurted out one day, as he was trying to explain why his meditation and yoga practice are so important to him. "I couldn't live and I couldn't die." That's when I understood. Meditation saved his life. It isn't a passion; it isn't an obsession. It is his salvation.

So I am intrigued by the chance to go out on a long walk with Juan. I'd love to hear his story. What is it about this world that he couldn't live in it? What does he do for a living? How did he discover meditation? I have so many questions.

Once we get past the monkey and the scooters and the apparent swami with the wild hair, I use my pastoral skills to try to get him talking.

"So, Juan, do you have family back in Spain?"

"Yeah, sort of." The way he says it tells me I should not ask him what "sort of" means.

"When did you first come to India?" I try another approach.

"Seven years ago." He doesn't elaborate, but he also doesn't close the door, so I keep trying.

"What brought you here?"

"Yoga and meditation." Hmmmm… Come on Juan, give me something to work with!

"What got you started with meditation?"

"Too many bad feelings. Too many bad thoughts." I get it. I also get that he doesn't want to tell me about the bad feelings and the bad thoughts, or his family that is only "sort of," or anything about his past. I stop trying.

We walk in silence. Once he realizes I'm not going to hound him with more questions, Juan is ready to talk. Out of nowhere, he comes out with his statement. "Three hours and eighteen minutes of perfect stillness leads to *Samadhi*."

"Three hours and eighteen minutes," I repeat back to Juan. "Really?" By now I should not be surprised by anything Juan might say. But I'm still not expecting to learn that the secret to enlightenment can be pinned down to a specific number of minutes.

"It's true," he insists. "I went to a talk by a swami, and he explained it. The mind is like water, and the body is like a glass containing the water. As long as the glass is moving, the water keeps sloshing around. But if the glass—the body—is still for long enough, eventually the water stops sloshing and the mind becomes still. Three hours and eighteen minutes. Then you achieve perfect peace."

I don't know what to say.

Juan goes on. "That's why I practice my yoga so much, so my body will be strong enough to sit still for longer. Once I stayed perfectly still for two hours and eight minutes."

What is the longest time I have ever stayed completely still while meditating? I doubt I can even claim eight minutes as my record.

We continue on our way, the silence getting more comfortable the longer we walk. I can't stop thinking about Juan's comment. Three hours and eighteen minutes. If I give myself credit for the ability to sit perfectly still for eight minutes—a dubious claim—, that still leaves me three hours and ten minutes to go.

I feel like a meditation slacker. Here I've been meditating, off and on, for more than twenty years, and I am a hundred and ninety minutes short. Worse still, I seem to be making no progress.

I like to think of myself as a hard worker. When I was in school, every paper was turned in on time, well-thought-out, neatly typed. In my ministry, I take pride in knowing people can count on me. I don't like the idea of being a slacker at anything, not even meditation.

As we walk, I plot my "slacker-no-more" strategy. Of course I know I'll never make it to three hours and eighteen minutes of perfect stillness, and I'm not actually convinced I want to achieve *Samadhi*. What would I do after that? But surely, I think, I can get a little closer—nine minutes, then ten. Maybe even a half hour. Will the sloshing water get still enough in a half hour for it to matter?

As I silently talk myself into working harder at my meditation, I feel something sink inside of me. What I treasure about meditation is that, for a half hour each day, I have permission not to accomplish anything. I don't have to solve a problem, although it's amazing how often unexpected solutions emerge from the silence. I'm not trying to write a sermon, though sometimes I get up from my meditation with just the right image to get me started. I'm not checking things off my to-do list, but in the silence I frequently remember something to add to it. Whether my mind races or floats or rests its way through that half hour, there is tremendous freedom in knowing I don't have to accomplish a thing.

Juan interrupts my internal debate. "I'm hot," he says. He points to a pickup truck approaching. "Let's get a ride on that truck."

I imagine Sister Tureeya's reaction if she learns I've been sitting in the back of a pickup truck with a bunch of men. I smile. "Sure, let's do it."

Juan waves the truck down. "Can you give us a ride into town? How much?"

"Thirty rupees," the driver smiles as he says it.

"Thirty," Juan glares at him. "That's too much."

"Okay twenty," the driver shrugs and starts the truck back up, ending the negotiations. We climb into the back.

Juan is still muttering under his breath about the twenty rupees we've been charged when we arrive at the market, but he cheers up when he sees his favorite fruit juice vendor. We hop out of the truck, and he approaches an old man with an even older-looking juicing machine.

"Two," he says gallantly.

I know this violates all the rules about safe eating for delicate American digestive systems—unfiltered water, raw fruit, an open air market. But there is no way I will turn down Juan's generosity.

We drink our pomegranate juice and hand the glasses back to the vendor to be reused. "We'd better hurry," Juan says, "Mataji will be mad if we're late for meditation."

Sister Tureeya is already seated on her cushion when Juan and I climb the stairs into the chapel at 2:57. Juan sits right down and immediately finds his meditation posture—legs twisted around each other to form that steady base he likes, back perfectly straight. More tentatively, I lower myself down to my cushion and try to arrange my legs into a comfortable position. My knees are sore from the dawn and noontime meditations. No matter how I shift my weight, I still feel my left ankle digging into my right leg—or my right ankle digging into my left leg. I lean slightly against the wall to keep my back sort-of-straight and try to focus on my breath and ignore my aching knees, my sharp ankle bones and my sagging back.

I breathe in and out. I repeat my mantra with every exhale. I shift my legs again in search of a more comfortable position. I straighten my flagging back. So much for eight minutes of perfect stillness; I am having trouble with eight seconds! The water in my glass is sloshing away, picking up speed with every splash.

These waters are alive!

I almost laugh out loud in the deadly-silent

meditation room as I finally get the joke. Of course these waters are alive; I have come to stay at the Jeevan Dhara ashram, the place of Living Waters. I squirm again on my cushion and revel in the waters sloshing against the glass, sloshing until they flow over the edge, bathing my whole being with grace.

My knees ache. My back aches. My mind flits around. And in it all, I feel a hint of peace. This peace doesn't come as a result of how hard I am working at my meditation. It certainly doesn't come from my sitting perfectly still. This peace is a gift.

Sister Tureeya is right after all. It is all about grace. Grace—God's free gift of love—bathes me with peace. Living water overflows in my life—not because of anything I do, not because I am good. Grace is a gift, given beyond all the distinctions of good and bad, deserving and undeserving.

My conversation with Juan almost seduced me. I came close to swallowing the old familiar poison—the intoxicating and ultimately deadly poison of trying to earn God's love. It's the poison that, twenty-two years ago, led me to meditate on the roof of the first Jeevan Dhara ashram with such determined intensity that I never saw the mountain peaks emerge.

No, I tell myself as I lean more heavily against the wall. No three hours and eighteen minutes of perfect stillness for me. No slacker-no-more strategizing. Just be still—or sort of still, still enough to receive this gift. Just sit under the waterfall. I give myself permission. Let the sloshing water overflow.

I open my eye for a moment and see Juan sitting perfectly still in his lotus position. Meditation saves Juan's life, slowing the sloshing down to a tolerable level, holding out hope that he will be able to live in this world. Meditation doesn't save my life. It opens me to what does, slowing me down enough to receive the free gift of God's love—unearned and unearnable—poured out on me like living water.

✸ Thursday ✸
"Immersion"

There are no familiar hymns to stir my homesickness at this worship service. There is very little, in fact, that feels familiar at all.

It is Maundy Thursday, sometimes called Holy Thursday—the day we remember Jesus' Last Supper with his disciples, his betrayal by a friend, and his arrest that leads to his crucifixion. Back home, I imagine, the people of my church are seated around tables in the fellowship hall, sharing a meal of bread, fruit and cheese before the lights go out and they tell the story once again. With each reading, another candle is extinguished. They will leave in darkness and silence.

Here there are no tables to sit around. There are no chairs either. I sit on the floor beside Sister Tureeya on the women's side of the only Christian church in Rishikesh. There are a few pillows scattered around, so I grab two, vaguely aware that I am taking more than my share. I try to arrange them so I can pretend to be comfortable for the next few hours. Without a wall to lean against, I suspect this will be even harder than meditation in the Jeevan Dhara chapel.

Even the priest doesn't get a chair. He sits facing us in the front of the sanctuary, behind a low communion table. The service begins with music and scripture, read by a series of men and boys. It is in Hindi, but I assume I am hearing the same texts we read every year back home. Unlike what I heard and sang at the Church of North India in New Delhi, the music has a distinctively Indian feel, almost like the songs and chants I remember from Hindu ashrams twenty-two years ago, and from Indian restaurants at home.

Early in this trip, Fran and I spent a week at the United Theological College in Bangalore, a seminary of the Church of South India. There we attended chapel services conducted by students who were seeking to enculturate Christianity—to separate the message of the Gospel from Western European and American trappings and express it in ways that honor the many diverse cultures of India. One young man produced a CD of *bhajans,* Christian hymns in the style of Hindu devotional music. It seemed a lively and fairly new enterprise.

As I rearrange myself on my pillows and listen to the *bhajans* in this service, I think about how far this Rishikesh church has come reshaping worship to be more expressive of the rich culture of India. Then I realize that it may not be a reshaping at all. It is not that they have ceremoniously removed the pews; more likely, the church never had them.

This church traces its roots to biblical times. According to tradition, the apostle usually called Doubting Thomas recovered from his moment of questioning to travel to South India, to what is now the state of Kerala, to proclaim the good news. When Western missionaries came to India many centuries later, they were surprised to find there were already Christians here, who had developed practices and rituals of their own. I find myself thinking about the young men and women at United Theological College who are working hard to reclaim Christianity in an Indian context. I wonder whether this particular church has also needed to work hard at that, or whether they are simply living the traditions they have inherited.

I recognize the basic elements of the service. After the music, scriptures and a sermon, twelve men and boys come forward to have the priest wash their feet, a ritual recalling how Jesus washed the disciples' feet. We all come forward for Communion, the male side of the room first, followed by the women and girls. We sit in silence for what Sister Tureeya whispers is a time for venerating the remaining

Communion wafers, and then they are placed in the tabernacle and removed from the church.

The scripture is read in Hindi and the sermon is in Malayalam, the language of the South Indian state of Kerala, from which many of the worshippers originally came. I try to stay present to the moment and to the story I assume is being told. Still, I have plenty of time to gaze at the artwork adorning the front of the sanctuary.

The first thing I notice is a brilliantly colored painting on the ceiling—a white dove surrounded by the colors of the rainbow. Just below the dove, on the front wall of the sanctuary, is a stunning work of art. The center of the piece is made of copper. The raised design reveals a man emerging out of a river. There are several other figures in the piece: a few people watching from a distance, and another man up close, holding a staff with a cross on it. The art extends beyond the copper sculpture, widening into a mosaic of blue and green tiles, creating the appearance of waves. The dove on the ceiling dominates the scene, descending upon the man in the center of the copper piece. It is the baptism of Jesus.

As the priest continues his reflections in Malayalam, I take a closer look. On either side of the river, pounded out in raised copper, are temples, shaped much like the Hindu temples that dominate the town of Rishikesh. This, I realize, is not the River Jordan in rural Galilee; it is the Ganges in Rishikesh. In Hinduism, bathing in the Ganges is an act of great religious merit. Pilgrims travel from all over India to do so. What is this painting saying about Jesus and his baptism? What does it mean to imagine Jesus baptized in the Ganges River, a pilgrim among pilgrims? No longer is the story about something that happened long ago in a distant land; it is a story happening right now, in the river down the hill.

Since I can't understand the sermon, I let my mind wander down that hill, back to the holy river—the river where Maria and I tossed water in the air for a blessing, the river Juan and I walked along, the river where my Haridwar Express seat-mate was going rafting. I remember my own attempt to bathe in this same river on my first trip to India, 22 years ago.

"You need to go to Rishikesh," Molly and Dick Turner, my very generous hosts in New Delhi, tell me. "If you want to see what ashram life is like, that's a good place to start. It's a holy city because it is on the holy river, the Ganges." Their neighbor, Sita, a young graduate student, has already taken me to Varanasi, the holiest of the cities along the river. We don't consider bathing there. The river is lined with funeral pyres; the ashes are released into the water.

"This is a sacred place," Sita says, "but don't get into the water; it is full of disease." She continues. "When you go to Rishikesh, the water is okay there. It is upstream."

Sita can't come with me on this trip to Rishikesh, so Molly helps me make arrangements. "We should write to Sivananda's ashram," she suggests. "They have lots of foreign visitors, so it'll be safe for you, and they'll speak English." We write to make arrangements, and when I get a confirmation back, Molly and I buy my train ticket, and I am off.

Sivananda's ashram, I read in my Lonely Planet guide, is famous—the headquarters of the Divine Life Society, home of one of the first Peace Poles. Sure enough, in the central courtyard I find the Sivananda Pillar, inscribed with his twenty spiritual instructions and sayings from many world religions.

Molly is right: Sivananda's ashram is accustomed to accommodating foreigners. In fact, they have a separate dormitory for us, with the rules written on the back of the doors in English, German and Spanish.

My concrete-block-mate is a young woman from Australia. Like many young people I meet from Australia and Europe, Tina is taking a year off after university to travel around the world.

Unlike me, she doesn't have a project; this trip is pure adventure. She is free.

It is my first taste of ashram life. The wake up bell rings at 4:30 am. There is yoga, meditation, breakfast, service, lunch, rest, more meditation, more yoga, supper, a talk and time for bed. I dive into the routine.

During the afternoon rest time, I meet with one of the swamis. "I'm working on a project," I explain, "trying to study the empowerment of women who come to ashrams."

The swami is very patient with me, and he very patiently declines to engage in the conversation I want to have. His purpose is different.

"It's not about empowerment," he explains. "It's about awakening."

"What do you mean?"

"Awakening, enlightenment—discovering our oneness with God."

"But I'm curious about how their time in the ashram changes the lives of the women when they return home."

"That's not what it's about." He is persistent. "It's about oneness. Brahman and Atman are one. The universal soul and your soul—they are one. It is all one."

"But I'm asking a different question. Maybe it's more of a sociological question than a theological question." I am as persistent as he is.

"It's the wrong question. There are no questions—only awakening."

He won't budge, but apparently I don't annoy him too much. He offers to meet with me the next day, and the next, and the next.

Meanwhile, Tina chafes at the restrictions of ashram life. "Early to bed and early to rise" is not the preferred lifestyle of a young world traveler. Occasionally she offers to lead me astray.

"Some of us are going to skip lunch and go to the river. We heard there's a place a few miles upstream with a huge rock. You can jump off. Want to come?"

I decline. "I don't have a bathing suit."

"I don't either. Who needs one? When you send clothes out for laundering, where do you think they're washed? In the river. I'm just going to jump in with my clothes on. They'll dry quickly."

I try another objection. "Do they really let people jump off the rock? Isn't it dangerous?"

"Maybe," she admits. "But I'm a strong swimmer."

I like to think of myself as a strong swimmer too. But I don't want to go. "Isn't it sacrilegious? Don't you think people will be offended?"

Tina isn't concerned about that. But she gets the message—I don't want to go. She and her world traveler friends go off to the river, and I go to argue with the swami.

A few days later, all the foreigners in the ashram receive notice that we will need to leave. A conference is coming in. We can stay in the hostel across the street and participate in the programs, but there is no room for us in the dormitory.

I go to my swami. "But I've been working hard, attending all the programs, meeting with you. And my confirmation letter says I can stay through next week."

He is sympathetic, but once again he won't budge. "If this is important to you, you can stay at the hostel and still meet with me and do all this work you've been doing."

Tina takes off, headed for her next adventure. I swallow my pride and check into the hostel across the street.

I am hurt by what feels like a snub from the ashram, and I feel a little rebellious. That afternoon, I take a walk upstream to see if I can find the giant rock. I find it, and immediately know I will never jump off. My decision has nothing to do with reverence for the river as a sacred Hindu pilgrimage site. That rock is way too high.

I find a lower, flat rock. I lie down and soak in the sun. When I get too hot, I decide to take a dip. "I'm not going swimming," I tell myself. "That might be sacrilegious. I'm bathing in the holy river. It's part of my research."

My rock juts out into the river to create what seems like a protected little cove. Gingerly, I slip down the rock into that cove. Immediately, the water grabs hold of me, trying to pull me under. I panic, imagining myself drawn out of the cove into the center of the river and the rapid current. Just before my head goes under, I grasp the rock and drag myself out.

Safe above the water, I allow my breath and my heart to return to normal. I watch the river with new appreciation. The current is strong. Far more dangerous, though, are the twists and swirls, the whirlpools that seem to appear in a random fashion. The mini-cove, I now see, is full of them, and so is the entire river. I sit until my clothes are dry and head back to the hostel across from the ashram, back to the safety of the daily routine.

The priest is still talking in Malayalam. I gaze at the art work, wishing I could get up from my double-cushion to get a closer look. I study the copper and the tile. Are there whirlpools hidden amongst the waves of the Ganges? I don't know if the artist intended them, but I imagine I can see them.

I also begin to imagine the scene and the story in a new way. I've always thought of Jesus' baptism as an act of will—his will, his decision to enter the water, his choice to plunge himself under, guided by the fiery John the Baptist. But the Ganges River, at least by the famous leaping rock, adds another element. Current drags you off balance. Whirlpools grab at you and pull you under. Yes, it is a choice to enter the river, to slide down the rocks or, in Jesus' case, to walk into the center. But when you least expect it, a whirlpool may drag you under. Unless you grab at a rock and pull yourself to safety, the water takes over. You are no longer in charge. You emerge sputtering, gasping for breath. More importantly, you emerge with a heightened sense of your vulnerability, your smallness in the face of forces beyond your control, your need for help. You emerge awakened to how fragile you are, how fragile this precious gift of human life is.

Sitting on my cushions staring at this stunning work of art, I silently recreate the story of Jesus' baptism—this time a Ganges River baptism. Jesus walks into the river, yearning for the renewal John the Baptist promises. Before he can decide whether he really wants to be made new, a whirlpool grabs hold of him and drags him under. He emerges, but only because his friend John extends a hand and pulls him out of the vortex.

Jesus is shaken. Any illusions he has about his own strength are shattered. Now he knows he cannot do it alone. Now he understands how desperately he needs God. In that moment, something changes in how he perceives himself. Even more, something changes in how he perceives the people around him. His compassion awakens—compassion for those whose need is out there in the open for everyone to see, for those whom life has dragged under. That awakening opens his eyes, and he sees the Holy Spirit descending upon him like a dove. It opens his ears, allowing him to hear the voice no one else can hear: "You are my child, my beloved."

It's not how I ever pictured Jesus' baptism before. It rings true to me, though, as I sit in church on Maundy Thursday, listening to the priest talk in Malayalam. I know he is telling the story of Jesus' Last Supper with his disciples, his betrayal by a friend, his anguish in the Garden of Gethsemane, the end of a ministry that began with his baptism. It is such a painfully human story. The artwork in front of me fits the occasion: Jesus' baptism as his awakening to his humanness—his human vulnerability, his human need, his human compassion. Jesus' baptism in the roiling waters of the Ganges is his baptism into the struggles and fears and worries of human living.

Living waters—Jeevan Dhara—flowing, swirling, twisting, pulling Jesus under, awakening him to the fear and need and compassion that shape human living.

I think back to my own awakening yesterday, in the stark meditation room of Jeevan Dhara ashram, living waters washing over me with the gift of grace. Are the living waters of the Ganges also a gift of grace? Is it grace that drags me away from the safety of the rock, from the comfort of familiar ways? Is it grace that awakens me to my need and to my kinship with the most vulnerable among us? Is it grace that places a little boy in front of me on the sidewalk in New Delhi and will not let me pass by? Could it be grace that will not let me forget his eyes?

I am much more comfortable when I choose to stay on that nice warm rock, when I succeed in dodging the child begging on the sidewalk. It is a comfort, though, that makes my life a little smaller. I am terrified of being pulled under by the waters, and I am terrified of what that little boy's eyes demand of my life.

Beneath that terror is my struggle to believe that when I am most vulnerable, I am most open to the Spirit. Deeper than that terror is my yearning to trust that recognizing a begging child's humanity makes me more fully human. Beyond the terror is faith that baptism is not just being pulled under but also arising to new life.

Living water, poured out on me like a waterfall, assures me that I am beloved. Living water, pulling me under like a whirlpool, awakens me to my need for love.

✷ Friday ✷
"Good After All"

What's so good about Friday anyway? It isn't even breakfast time, and I am already hungry. Last night, Sister Tureeya announced we would fast on Good Friday, until supper time. I sit in the pre-dawn dark of the stark meditation room, imagining that I can already hear my stomach growling, if only in anticipation of hunger that will be.

Back home I never fast on Good Friday; I need all the strength my breakfast can give me. I generally spend the morning running around, coordinating last-minute details for an ecumenical worship service, with participation from multiple denominations.

Good Friday is a complicated day to hold an ecumenical service. The story we tell that day is one Christians, from the very beginning of our faith, have struggled to understand. What does it mean when the person you thought would save you dies a criminal death? The writings of the early church reflect a stunning diversity of ideas as they grappled with the meaning of a crucified savior. In the millennia that have followed, still more images and explanations evolved. The churches in Framingham, Massachusetts—and their pastors—reflect some of that diversity. There are liberal Protestants and Evangelicals, progressive Catholics and their more traditional counterparts. There are folks who trace their roots to the Puritans and others who learned to preach in the African-American tradition.

For years, one of the mainstays of the service was Bob, pastor of the Assemblies of God Church. A short man with a mustache, a booming voice, and a twinkle in his eye, Bob was a proud Fundamentalist, an eager participant in all things ecumenical, and an enthusiastic actor. Bob would enter into whatever role he'd selected—King Herod, a thief on a cross, a renegade Centurion—with gusto. His portrayals frequently brought the house down, if it's possible to bring down a Good Friday house. I never knew quite what he was going to say. Not knowing made me nervous.

So back home I don't fast on Good Friday. If anything I have extra protein with my breakfast. I know I'll need every ounce of energy to manage this service, or maybe just to manage my own discomfort with such a brutal and bloody story.

This year, I have no reason to avoid fasting. There

is nothing for me to manage but my own discomfort. I have not been part of a planning team, and there will be no opportunity to shape the service to suit my own theology. Of course, since I won't understand any of the words being spoken, I will be free to imagine whatever I want.

A few minutes before noon, Sister Tureeya and I head downtown for church. The growling in my stomach is no longer a figment of my imagination. The service begins like yesterday's. We sit on the floor on the women's side, and listen to what I assume is a reading of the passion story. Once again, all the readers are men and boys. We have communion with the host that was consecrated at yesterday's service. I sit with my back sagging, trying to stay focused on the story I know so well that I don't need to speak Hindi.

"Come on, let's go." Sister Tureeya whispers as she nudges me. It seems too soon for the service to be over. "Come on, get up, we're going outside for the Stations of the Cross." She whispers from between her teeth. "I don't know why he insists on doing it outside. It's not safe."

Not safe? We follow the crowd out into the compound. The walls are high; no one can see what we are doing. What can be unsafe about a bunch of church people walking around church property? I feel a flash of anger. Rishikesh is full of public displays of religiosity—gurus on the corner, altars by the side of the road, flyers and banners and yogis of all kinds. What is wrong with our very quiet display, in our own walled compound, on one of the holiest days of the Christian year?

I hear the priest's voice as he begins the prayers for the first station, but I am too far back to see either him or the picture, representing the station, which is mounted on the compound wall. The men left the church first; they are all in front. The women and girls are in the back. Finally, as we parade past it on the way to the next station, we catch a quick glimpse—a beaten-down Jesus and an arrogant Pilate. Following behind the men, we make our way around the compound—16 stations, 16 after-the-fact glimpses for the women. Then the service is over.

As we walk back to the ashram I ask Sister Tureeya why she fears it is unsafe to do the Stations of the Cross outside. She shushes me sharply. "Later," she hisses.

When we get back to the ashram I try again. "It doesn't make sense," I begin. "There are all sorts of religious processions going on all the time in Rishikesh. Why should it be dangerous to have an outdoor Stations of the Cross?"

"It's our own fault." Sister Tureeya's response is almost a retort. "We brought it on ourselves."

She continues. "For so long Christians pretended we were better than everyone else. Because of the missionaries and their connections with the colonial powers, Christian churches had land and built schools and hospitals. Everyone needed us, and we used that to try to convert them. Now things are different. There are other schools and other hospitals, so they don't need us anymore.

"Everyone complains about the rise of Hindu Fundamentalism," she goes on, "but we forget that for most of our history here, Christians were the Fundamentalists. Now we're getting a dose of our own medicine."

I feel the bitterness rising up in Sister Tureeya's words. She has thought deeply about this. She is passionate about finding a different way. No one, it seems, is listening to her.

She gives me her prescription for the church: "The church needs to get off its high horse and out of the bishops' houses. The priests need to get out of their cassocks and into traditional Indian clothes. We need to create ashrams and give the schools to the lay people to run."

She isn't done yet. "What Christianity in India needs—and what Hindu people need to see in order to respect Christians—is renunciation." She describes the way the connection to the colonial powers has poisoned the broader culture's view of Christianity. "The church," she says, "must give up the trappings of success—that means our land and our schools and hospitals. Even more," she elaborates, "Christians need to develop disciplined spiritual practices. We need meditation, renunciation, silence." I've heard this before…

No wonder Sister Tureeya is so bitter; disappointment comes at her from all sides. She firmly believes that what Christianity needs is more ashrams, but the one she leads appears to be dying. She is passionate that Christians need disciplined spiritual practices, but her sole ashram resident, whose disciplined spiritual practices outshine even hers, is often hostile to Christianity.

As if on cue, Juan comes through the compound door, back from an extended yoga class. I am tired of Sister Tureeya's rant and tired of sitting still. I figure that, if I am going to be hungry anyway, I might as well get out. "Feel like a walk?" I ask Juan. There will be no afternoon meditation and no tea time today, so we are free.

Juan smiles broadly, and we set off. As before, we head across the monkey-laden bridge and up the road paralleling the river. This time, Juan guides me down a steep embankment until we come to a rocky beach beside the Ganges. We wander in silence along the river, stepping gingerly on the piles of smooth round stones. Up ahead a pile of granite rock grabs our attention. The square corners and crisp edges seem out of place beside the smooth river stones. A human addition, no doubt. Maybe leftovers dumped from a construction project.

Without speaking, Juan strides over to the stones. He bends down and erects a cross. It is, after all, Good Friday. Once again, Juan has left me speechless. I take a picture of the cross and its creator, and we amble on.

Later, back on the road, Juan grows uncharacteristically talkative. He starts telling me about the yogis he admires. "The most advanced ones," he says, "have so much spiritual power no one can harm them. Even weapons are repelled."

Good Friday is still on his mind. "That's what I don't get about Jesus. If he had so much spiritual power, how could those people hurt him?" He offers his own answer: "I think he must not have been so powerful."

He pauses a moment. "I know they say he chose not to use his power." I hear his skepticism. "They say he had to die to save us from our sins."

I flash back to Good Friday at home, to our assiduous efforts to avoid the conversation we fear will tear our ecumenical Good Friday tradition apart, to my cautious friendship with Pastor Bob. "Jesus died to save us from our sins," Juan says. What does that mean? Should I go there?

In a moment of courage that might be mistaken for fool-hardiness, I decide to leap in. I take a deep breath. "I don't think Jesus died as a sacrifice for our sins."

By now we are walking along the road. Juan stops short. "What?" He looks shocked. For someone who complains that Christianity is all about dogma, Juan suddenly becomes quite dogmatic. "I thought you were a Christian."

"I am." I am feeling a little defensive.

"Isn't that what Christians are supposed to believe? That's what my priest taught me. I thought you were kind of like a priest."

I'm beginning to regret my moment of courage. How can I explain what I can barely make sense of myself?

"It doesn't make sense to me—this sacrifice idea," I begin. "We say God is all-powerful…"

"Right." Juan looks dubious. "So?"

"So if God is all-powerful, why would God need to sacrifice Jesus in order to forgive us? Why couldn't God just forgive?"

"I thought that was the way it worked. I thought those were the rules." Now Juan looks even more dubious.

"Whose rules?"

"I thought they were God's rules." In spite of his tea-time objections to the very notion of Christian theology, Juan is determined to defend this particular version of it.

"That doesn't make sense to me either." I'm on a roll, though I'm not sure where I'm rolling. Maybe over a cliff… "God is love—for me that's the bottom line. Sacrificing Jesus seems like the opposite of love."

Juan is silent, thinking. I am silent, waiting and preparing for the question I am sure is coming, "Then why did Jesus die on a cross?" It's Good Friday, after all; it's the question of the day.

When Juan finally speaks, he doesn't ask the question I am preparing to answer. Instead, he goes back to his yogis and their powers. "So I was right from the start. Jesus couldn't stop all those people from hurting him. He's not nearly as powerful as those yogis I was telling you about. Why would you follow someone who doesn't even have enough spiritual power to save himself? I don't understand why you'd want to be a Christian."

This time I'm the one who stops short on the road. "Juan, that's the point! That's why I am a Christian!"

He looks at me as though a crazy person has taken over his friendly fellow-ashramite. "Now you don't make any sense at all," he blurts out.

I know he's right—it doesn't make any sense. And I stand by my words. I try again. "Jesus was powerful, only it was a different kind of power."

"What do you mean?" Juan is genuinely interested, and he's utterly confused. I understand why.

The yogis Juan admires practice their spiritual disciplines with such rigor that not even weapons can harm them. Presumably, that means they have the power to protect themselves from all the other dangers that plague ordinary human beings. If they can repel weapons, they can repel jealousy and hatred, grief and depression. Surely they are free from the ravages of cancer—and even the annoyance of the common cold.

Juan's gurus have a seductive appeal to me, kind of like the seductiveness of achieving enlightenment in 3 hours and 18 minutes. There's something alluring about the notion that if I work hard enough at my spiritual practices I can achieve enlightenment—and also invulnerability. Pretty quickly, for me, the appeal reveals its emptiness. I'm certain I will never be able to sit still for three hours and 18 minutes. I'm even more certain I will never develop the spiritual power to repel weapons. More importantly, I'm not sure I really want to.

Of course I want to be in control of my life, and I might even like to be invulnerable. But there are other things I want more. I want genuine human connection, and the only way that happens is if we need each other. I long to experience tenderness, and that only comes if I risk opening up to my own weakness. I yearn to feel compassion, and so I must draw upon my own experience of pain and loss in order to touch someone else's. Connection, tenderness, compassion—they are inextricably tied up with vulnerability. As much as I'd like to be completely in charge of my life, to be invulnerable, I want connection, tenderness and compassion more.

To be human is to live with a mix of so many contradictory realities—power and powerlessness, miraculous bodies that betray us, fear and courage, deep love that falls short. Sometimes that complicated mix is so painful I long for a savior to swoop down and rescue me from my humanness—or at least a super-yogi who can teach me to achieve my own self-rescue. Most of the time, though, I don't want to escape.

I don't need a savior to rescue me from being human. I need a savior to free me from the traps that keep me from savoring my humanness. I need a savior who embraces that complicated mix of human living so fully that I am inspired to embrace it myself. I need a savior who teaches me that God treasures all of who I am. And I need a savior who reminds me that it is not all about me.

How do I explain to Juan why a super-yogi can't be my savior? I struggle for some way to get past all the theological words. Suddenly I know what I need to say—for myself if not for him.

"So Juan, last Sunday I was in New Delhi and I was walking down the street. A little boy—he was just a kid and his clothes and his face were filthy—he stopped me to ask for *baksheesh*. I said no, and I tried to walk around him, but he wouldn't let me. He spread his arms out like this—" I demonstrate, "like a cross."

"What happened?" I have Juan's full attention now.

"An auto rickshaw driver stopped and made him go away."

Juan looks relieved.

"And that's when I got it. Jesus isn't the auto rickshaw driver, saving me from that situation, protecting me from feeling so awful about not doing anything to help the little boy. Jesus is that little boy—Jesus on the cross."

I realize then that I am still standing there with my arms outstretched—my own cross. I feel a little embarrassed as I lower them. But I'm too far along to stop. "I really wanted the little boy to go away. Sometimes I wish Jesus would save me from all the pain of the world. But that's not what salvation means. Jesus faces me down on the street and refuses to let me escape. Jesus doesn't save me from the world; Jesus saves me to be in the world in a new way."

"What way?"

"The way that makes me want to do something to make the world better. The way that won't let me forget that little boy until he doesn't have to beg anymore. The way of compassion."

I pause for breath. Juan waits. "That's what I meant when I said that Jesus had—well, has—a different kind of power. Jesus' power is to show us that the weakest, most vulnerable person is holy. To show that, he had to be vulnerable too, human like us. Maybe he even needed to die—because little boys like the one who accosted me die too young. It's an upside-down power. To be powerful he had to be vulnerable."

Now I'm really embarrassed. I'm not sure this is what Juan bargained for when he agreed to go on a walk with me. I look at him. "Does that sort of make sense?"

He looks back at me and smiles. "I think you are the strangest Christian I have ever met." From Juan, that is high praise.

Now I am ready to claim my answer to the question that started my day, "What's so good about Friday?" It's not Good Friday because Jesus suffered and died—that isn't good; in fact it's horrifying. What is good is that, through this story, we know that Jesus is not a super-yogi. We know that he shares our human reality: the beauty and pain of friendship, the joy of laughter and the sorrow of tears, possibility and failure, suffering and death. We know that God treasures the fullness of human living. Because we know that, we are saved for lives of connection, tenderness and compassion. Surely that is good.

We walk on in silence. When we get back to the ashram, I pull my camera out of my pocket and scroll back to show Juan the picture I took: Juan standing beside the stone cross he constructed on the banks of the Ganges River. He smiles broadly. "I think it is a very nice cross."

I still don't understand what prompted Juan to pick up those stones and make them into a cross. I wonder—does he secretly long for a savior who will let him be human?

✶

✷ Saturday ✷
"A Dangerous Secret"

It is almost midnight when we leave the ashram, gingerly locking the steel gate behind us. Sister Tureeya motions for me to put my scarf over my head and to walk without scuffing my sandals, so as not to attract attention. We cross to the other side of the narrow alleyway, hoping the neighbor's dog won't smell us and start barking. When we hear two drunken men approaching, we creep into a vacant lot and pray they won't notice.

As we slink through the back alleys, I find myself thinking of the Easter story I know I will hear tomorrow, albeit in Hindi or Malayalam. I imagine the women in Mark's version of the story—Mary Magdalene, Mary the mother of James, and Salome—sneaking through the back alleys of Jerusalem before the break of dawn. They were on their way to anoint the body of their beloved friend and teacher Jesus. They went in secret, fully aware of the danger of being associated with this crucified rebel. Crucifixion was a brutal punishment Rome reserved for people they considered a threat to their power. They used it liberally, and publicly, to keep their subjects living in fear. How would the Romans—or religious leaders who were trying to appease the Romans—interpret the three women's refusal to abandon the body of their crucified friend?

The women weren't expecting a miracle; they took this risk simply out of love for their friend and loyalty to his teachings. Even before they discovered that his body was missing, their sneaking through the streets of Jerusalem enacted the message of the resurrection—Jesus' teaching about the power of God's love, which cannot be destroyed, not even by death. Love is stronger than hate and fear.

Sister Tureeya interrupts my silent imaginings by shushing me one more time. I must have scuffed my sandal on the sidewalk. Once more, I feel that sense of danger and secrecy. Ironically, for us tonight in Rishikesh, the danger is not because of authorities abusing their power to squelch a movement of liberation and love, but because of the long history of Christians abusing our power. The danger, at least as Sister Tureeya explained it yesterday, is the result of the ways Christianity in India lost sight of Jesus' message, the inevitable outcome when love becomes lost in the quest for control.

I think about the ways those of us who call ourselves liberal Christians sneak around back home. We don't literally have to tiptoe through back alleys to come to church—but sometimes we do the spiritual equivalent. We make sure people know we are not the kind of Christian that tries to impose our faith on other people. We avoid talking about Jesus so people don't stereotype us as close-minded or naïve. We slip through the streets hiding what, at least in theory, is at the center of our lives.

Finally, we get to the road. Sister Tureeya relaxes a bit, so I do too. We walk in silence until we arrive at the only lit building on the street. She opens the steel gate, a little less gingerly than she closed ours a few minutes ago. The atmosphere brightens as we enter the walled-in yard. With a tangible sense of relief, we greet the other worshipers who have come to church for the Easter vigil.

We join the congregation gathering outside in a clump, men on one side and women on the other. The priest speaks a few words I don't understand. A young man lights incense on a makeshift altar. And then—whoosh! Flames erupt in a fire pit constructed from a giant metal oil drum.

The wind whips through Rishikesh at night. With each gust, the fire threatens to escape the fire pit. Smoke blows in our faces. We rearrange ourselves, trying to avoid the shifting smoke, longing to feel the warmth of the fire, drawing back when the flames leap too close.

This, I think, is the real threat—not what Sister Tureeya perceives out on the street, certainly not my worries about how other people will interpret my faith. The danger is right here—a fire that cannot be contained by a fire pit, a faith that cannot be contained by all our efforts to make it safe and comfortable. The danger is the little boy on the street who refuses to let me pretend he doesn't exist. The danger is what will happen to our lives if we dare to believe the story we will proclaim tomorrow.

One of the boys starts passing around a box of candles. I take one and pass it on. A young man lights his candle from the fire and then holds it for an older man to light his.

Finally, something that feels familiar! I have led many candlelight services, usually on Christmas Eve. Back home, it is carefully managed. The liturgist and I light our candles from the Christ candle, then walk down the aisle together, stopping at each pew to light a worshiper's candle. They in turn light their neighbors' candles, all the way down the row. Everyone follows careful instructions for how to tilt the candles to avoid dripping wax on the pews. Our plastic candle-holders keep the wax from burning our hands. By the time we reach the back, the deacon has turned out all the electric lights, and the sanctuary is gently lit with candles. We watch the light of Christ grow—candle by candle, person by person, neighbors sharing the light with each other.

Like our Christmas Eve services back home, this Easter vigil involves sharing the light from a single flame. The similarity ends there. We aren't seated in neat rows for a nice orderly lighting; we are standing in a movable clump, huddled together as we try to stay warm and avoid the smoke and flames. There are no plastic candle holders to protect our hands.

And we are outside. The wind swirls around us, extinguishing our candles as quickly as we light them, occasionally threatening to set our headscarves ablaze. We light our candles, cup our hands around them as best we can, reach over to relight a neighbor's candle when we notice hers has gone out, nudge another neighbor for help when ours goes out, wince when hot wax makes it onto our hands. We laugh at the absurdity of our efforts, and we keep trying. There is never a moment when all the candles are lit, but at any given moment, someone is bearing the light.

It feels a little like the way a secret is shared—passed on from one person to another, lost at times in the winds of confusion and misunderstanding. This light we share, I know, isn't supposed to be a secret. It's meant to be a way of life, boldly proclaimed through our actions. In some ways it feels even more delicate than a secret, because even when we have known and believed it, we cannot always hold fast to it. As my candle is snuffed by a gust of wind yet again, I think about the winds of despair that can seem so overwhelming God's love appears to be an illusion. For those times, I need someone else to hold the light for me, until I find courage to relight my own candle. Other times, without realizing what I am doing, I lose sight of the realm of God's love and cast my lot with the powers of fear, or I pretend I can sit it out on the sidelines. In those times, I need a sister or brother in faith to hold out their candle, to shine a light on the path back to love and hope.

I stand with my candle extinguished for only a moment, and then, gratefully, I accept a silent offer—a young woman holds out her candle and I relight mine, cupping our hands to protect the transaction.

We stand for a while, lighting and relighting, then we parade around the yard, up to the doors of the church, where we deposit our by-now-extinguished candles in a tub of sand and come into the sanctuary.

As the service begins, Sister Tureeya leans over and whispers to me, "Tonight the service is all in Malayalam," the native language of most of the congregation. On this solemn night, when hope is a candle buffeted by the Rishikesh wind, the priest wants his congregation to feel at home. Sister

Tureeya is pleased, even though it means she won't understand the words any better than I will. The language makes a difference to the rest of the congregation. When it is time for a hymn, everyone sings with enthusiasm, even though it is the middle of the night.

A young woman comes forward and sings a haunting solo. It is the first time I have seen a woman participate in a service here. Is it the nighttime that allows some new openness to break through? Is it the promise that Easter will tear down all the divisions that keep us apart? The light from that delicate candle feels a little stronger.

After she finishes her solo, the young woman sits back down on the men's side. When it is time for communion, she goes first, along with the men. It's almost as though leading makes her an honorary man. So much, I think, for the promise that Easter breaks down all the barriers. I guess that's what we do: we light candles and allow the wind to snuff them out; we break down barriers and then set them up again. The question is whether we keep trying—to tear down walls, to re-light candles.

I wait my turn, go up to receive communion with the rest of the women—those of us who have not been made honorary men for the night—and sit back down on the floor for the final prayers. "Come on," Sister Tureeya says, "it's time to go."

We nod our farewells to the women sitting around us and go out into the cold courtyard, where the fire is still threatening the boundaries of the fire pit. Before she opens the metal gate to the street, she turns to remind me: "Shhhhh… Be quiet. Don't talk. Pick up your feet."

Once again, we sneak through the back alleys of Rishikesh, as though we are carrying a dangerous secret.

It is dangerous—a bonfire that threatens to break out of its fire pit, a message that promises to turn our world upside down. But it is not a secret—not as long as people gather together with their candles and offer to share the light they hold.

✴ Easter Sunday ✴
"Ice Cream at the Ashram"

The sun has risen. The tomb is empty. Christ is risen! Juan is coming to church!

I'm not sure why. Maybe Sister Tureeya told him it was an expectation: if you want to stay at a Christian ashram, you have to go to church on Easter. I don't think so. Juan doesn't have that sulky expression he gets when Sister Tureeya tells him to do something. I think he just decided to go—out of curiosity, or old habit from his Catholic upbringing, or feeling left out. Maybe it is an act of kindness; he knows it will make Sister Tureeya happy.

Whatever the reason, he has put on his best drawstring pants, a shirt with buttons and a Nehru collar, and he walks with us through the now brightly lit streets to the church. He sits in his best lotus position, back much straighter than mine, and acts interested through the entire service. What, I wonder, has happened to Juan?

The service begins with a baptism. The proud parents stand at the entrance to the church, where a simple wooden baptismal font has been placed. They are dressed in their Sunday best—a pinstripe Western-style suit and tie for the father, a shimmering gold and blue sari for the mother. The baby, held tenderly in her father's arms, is dressed in a flowing white silk baptismal gown.

The priest asks questions and the parents answer. Then he blesses the water, dips his fingers into the font and gently makes the sign of the cross on the little girl's forehead.

I turn my head, just for a moment, and look up at the mosaic and copper art at the front of the church: Jesus coming out of the churning Ganges River after his own baptism, guarded by a fierce-looking John the Baptist. I think about Jeevan Dhara and the living waters that slosh around inside me when I try to meditate—the fountain of grace that pours over me when I slow down enough to notice.

This baptism today is no roiling river, no overflowing fountain. It is just a few drops of water on a baby's forehead—gentle, tender, safe. Those few drops convey a river and a fountain of promise: a promise that, deep within this child, there is a stream of living water flowing to quench her thirst; a promise that God's grace will wash over her again and again; an assurance that when the swirling waters of life pull her under, she will emerge transformed.

After the baptism, the priest holds out a candle to the parents, who wrap the child's tiny hands around it, and then wrap their own hands around hers. The priest lights the wick.

It is the same kind of candle we lit and relit only a few hours ago, in the dark of the Easter vigil. This time, the candle stays lit. There are no winds to snuff it out. The parent's hands cover the child's: if wax drips, they will feel it but the baby will be protected.

I can't understand the words the priest says, but I do understand the message: the light of Christ is in this little girl. Her parents promise to hold the candle for her—with her—until her hands and her heart are mature enough that she can hold it herself. The church promises to bring her into the Easter vigil clump—to relight her candle every time the whipping winds of life snuff it out, and to call upon her to share her light with them and with the world.

The priest offers a prayer, takes the candle and places it, lit, in a bed of sand. The young family sits back down on the floor and the service proceeds: hymns, prayers, readings in Malayalam and Hindi, until it is time for the gospel.

A young woman, maybe Australian, walks up to the front of the church with a Bible in her hand and reads the Easter story in English. As we entered this morning, I noticed a few other folks who don't appear to be Indian in the church. Still, the vast majority of the congregation is from South India. They are hearing the gospel reading—certainly the most important reading of the service and probably the most important text of their Christian faith—in a foreign language. Some of them may understand it; others have to rely on already knowing the story.

English in India is a language of privilege and power—the language of the colonizer, the language of international business and middle-class success. Here, though, I think it is simply the language of the strangers.

Last night, the priest chose to conduct the service in Malayalam, as an affirmation of the worth of the vast majority of the people who gathered. Today, in celebration of how the resurrection changes everything, he has arranged to have the gospel read in English, so the five or six of us who are far from home will know we are welcome—included, part of the resurrection community. All the complicated history of English and Christianity in India, in this moment, matters less than the call to a radical act of hospitality. The call is inspired by a radical story of an empty tomb and a radical message that love is more powerful than anything that threatens to divide us.

The service ends. We greet our fellow worshipers more enthusiastically than usual and leave the compound. Sister Tureeya doesn't tell me to be quiet. Juan and I head to an Internet café that advertises cheap international calls, so I can call Fran for Easter. Before we leave, Sister Tureeya makes her announcement: "Today we will go out for lunch."

Juan and I almost fall over into the street. Ashramites don't usually go out for lunch. *Sannyasis*—Christian, Hindu, or otherwise—definitely don't go out for lunch. But it is Easter, and that's what we are going to do.

Juan and I place our calls, check our email and make sure to be back at the ashram in plenty of time. We don't want to be late for this momentous occasion.

Sister Tureeya has chosen the Children's Seva Mission for our outing. It is only a block from the ashram, but it feels worlds away. It is a funky, quasi-new age place that young world travelers frequent. If it had been around when I was in India as a 22-year-old, I would have hung out there between yoga classes.

The seats are wide benches built out from oddly-shaped alcoves. Brightly decorated cushions are tossed liberally around. The tables are unusual shapes, designed to fit neatly into the alcoves. A small library section contains inspirational literature, mostly in English or European languages. Another section displays earrings and hand-embroidered shawls for sale.

The literature on the lunch table reminds us that Children's Seva Mission is a charity. All proceeds from the restaurant and store go to support programs for street children in Rishikesh. *Seva* is a Sanskrit word that is most often translated as "service." One of the many spiritual paths in Hinduism is the path of *seva*. In doing service to others, as I understand it, we come to recognize our oneness with them—the first step toward awakening to the oneness of all creation, and our oneness with God.

Most of the waitresses at Children's Seva Mission appear to be those young world travelers—seekers who yearn to give something back. They are kind and friendly, and a little perplexed by this odd-looking threesome. I suspect Sister Tureeya is the first person wearing saffron robes who has ever come in as a paying customer.

We sit in our usual cross-legged positions—Juan in full-lotus, me in an off-centered half-lotus, and Sister Tureeya with her legs discreetly hidden beneath her robes. Only today we aren't sitting on the floor.

Sister Tureeya looks at the menu, asks about

our favorites, and then orders for us all. It is a feast. The food is part Indian and part international veggie-foodie. We have carrot soup, delicately flavored with ginger and coriander; saffron rice cooked in coconut milk; roasted vegetables in a spicy peanut sauce that seems more Thai than Indian. We drink mango *lassis*. There is hardly room for it all on our table.

We eat and eat. "Have more," Sister Tureeya prompts.

"I'm full," Juan protests.

I am full too, but I eat more. I don't want the food to go to waste. Even more, I want to honor whatever has prompted this act of abundance from our renunciate-leader.

The conversation is forced; Juan is largely uncommunicative. I think he is in shock. I suspect he is ambivalent about so much food: eating too much, he told me earlier in the week, reduces the power of meditation. I also think he doesn't know what to say. His familiar conversation pattern with Sister Tureeya is argument, and I imagine he doesn't want to spoil the moment by starting a fight. So he says nothing. I make a few attempts at casual conversation, then I give up and just enjoy the meal.

Before we are done, Sister Tureeya calls the waitress over and says she wants to order dinner to take back to the ashram. Another first. "The old man is away," she explains, "and I'm too tired to cook." She orders samosas, more saffron rice, and ice cream—the "nutty-buddy" cones they used to sell in my elementary school cafeteria.

I offer to help pay, but she brushes me off. We waddle back to the ashram. Sister Tureeya puts the already-melting ice cream cones in her mini-freezer, and we all return to our rooms to digest.

No one is hungry for dinner, but we dutifully show up and try to eat the now-soggy samosas and the refrozen ice cream. Juan is back to his usual self, talking about his goal of longer and deeper meditation, mastering his body and his thoughts. Sister Tureeya is back too, countering his vision with her sharp reminder that it is all about grace. I float an alternative, inspired by the Children's Seva Mission. "If we add *seva*—service—as a third possibility, could it be that we all have a primary way we seek our spiritual goals, but also need the other two to balance them?" They sink my trial balloon. "No, it's about grace." "No, it's about achieving perfect stillness." We are all back to our roles, but something is different tonight. We are eating ice cream at the ashram.

Juan and I collect the dishes. As we wash them, he whispers to me, "What has happened to Mataji?" It is the same question I asked myself about Juan this morning when I saw him all dressed up for church.

He goes on with his own explanation. "She must like you a lot." Maybe that is part of it. She knows I am leaving the next day, and maybe she is just expressing her gratitude that someone has come to her ashram for its intended purpose.

I choose to interpret it differently. I think she got it—Easter, that is. At least for that lunch and maybe even for that dinner, Sister Tureeya allowed the story of Easter to change her. She recognized that the good news is such good news that we simply have to celebrate. It is such good news that the rules for ashram living have to be broken, if only for a day. It is such good news that we need a feast, a tasty expression of God's abundance. We need to enact all those favorite Bible passages about cups running over and tables overflowing.

We have been eating together for the entire week, but this eating together is different. The shared meal at the Children's Seva Mission is an expression of our faith that the resurrection is not just about new life for each of us as individuals. It is about new life together—community.

The awkwardness of our meal is a vivid reminder that Easter doesn't turn us into perfect human beings or perfectly harmonious communities. We still bring our old hurts, deep needs, and conflicting theories to the table. But Sister Tureeya lets go of her need to argue about grace long enough to receive it and offer it. Juan lets go of his yearning for perfect peace long enough to enjoy this taste of peace. I let go of my judgments about both of them long enough to appreciate sharing a meal with them, just as they are. We are a small, awkward Easter community, celebrating the good news of hope and new life.

My Holy Week began in New Delhi, as I sat in a pew in an English-speaking church, weeping at the sound of familiar hymns. It ends in Rishikesh, as I sit on the floor in a Hindi-Malayalam-speaking church, in awe at the story told in English so the strangers will know we belong.

My Holy Week began with a desperate little boy holding his arms out to block my path, Christ crucified on a New Delhi sidewalk. It ends with a celebration of the light of Christ in a baby girl, and with a meal in a restaurant dedicated to making sure other little boys and girls won't need to beg.

My Holy Week began with a dream of returning to an ashram paradise of my memories—a place of natural beauty, deep transformation, gentle community. It ends with ice cream at an ashram that is a long way from paradise. It ends with a recognition that beauty is hidden amidst the ordinary and the frustrating, and that most of us are wise and foolish both at the same time. It ends with a renewed understanding that transformation is usually slow and often painful, and that community requires tremendous patience and forbearance.

Along the way, I rediscover the promise that Christ shares in all the messy complexities of our human living. Along the way, I come to celebrate that it is all holy.

✷ Easter Mondays ✷
"The Journey Continues"

Holy week is over. I am planning to leave Jeevan Dhara after lunch. This morning, at breakfast, Sister Tureeya has an idea. "We haven't had a priest here at the ashram in so long, so we haven't been able to celebrate mass here in our chapel. You're an ordained minister. You could consecrate the host."

"Sure," I say. "I would love to serve communion." I'm pleased to be asked but a little confused. "You know I'm not Catholic."

"That doesn't matter." Sister Tureeya is not to be deterred. "You're a minister, so you can do it. Right?"

"Right."

"We have a beautiful Communion liturgy in our prayer book. You should use that." She says it as though it is decided.

While she and Juan clear the breakfast dishes, I look over the liturgy. She is right; it is beautiful. It also contains words I am pretty sure are intended to be said only by Catholic priests.

Remembering our meals yesterday, and the way Easter broke through the rules of ashram living, I decide we might as well break one more rule. So, before lunch, instead of our usual hour of meditation, we go into the chapel for communion. I use the beautiful words of the liturgy; I choose to trust that the intent of our prayers are more important than whether they are Catholic or Protestant words.

Sister Tureeya found some communion wine in the refrigerator, and we use a *chapatti* left over from breakfast. It feels like a parting gift to serve Sister Tureeya the bread of life, a way I can let her know that I honor her passion for what it means to be Christian in this broken world. It feels a little strange to serve Juan, who dutifully participates, because I'm not sure what it means to him. I choose to understand it as an expression of friendship. I choose to offer it as a prayer-in-bread-and-wine that somehow, through yoga and perfect stillness, through grace or even through companionship, he will awaken to the peace he so yearns to find.

Today there is no ice cream. Still, the feast continues.

❊ ❊ ❊

I return to New Delhi a few weeks later, after a trekking and rafting trip, which takes me, much to my surprise, down the Ganges River and right by the Leaping Rock. I do not jump off the rock.

On my last night in India, I stay at the New Delhi YMCA. After I settle into my room, I go to the front desk. "Is Mr. Samuel in?" I ask the young woman behind the counter.

"Mr. Samuel?" She looks puzzled. "Oh, he retired. His last day of work was last week. Why?"

"I have something for him. Do you have an address where I could mail it?"

She starts to look it up, and then she pauses. "He'll be back next week to pick up his last paycheck. Do you want to leave it for him?"

I pull out the envelope, which contains five 1000 rupee notes, write Addison Samuel on the front, and give it to the young woman. It is about $75, a night's stay at the Y for me, a month's rent for him.

I hope he gets it. I hope he isn't offended. I hope it helps.

❖ ❖ ❖

Two weeks after that, I am back at home, my sabbatical time over. I go back to work. I have hundreds of pictures for a slide show, lots of sermon illustrations, and even more to think about. Within a few months, I feel stuck. Something is missing. I begin to meet with a new spiritual director, and in the course of our conversations I discover what the barrier is.

Some years ago, I began working with a journaling technique that involved writing a dialogue with Jesus. I initially was reluctant to try that technique, thinking I would just be putting words in Jesus' mouth, remaking my savior in my own image. A friend encouraged me to try anyway, reminding me that the Holy One—God, Jesus, the Spirit—resides within us as well as around us. So I tried it, and I discovered that the words I wrote in Jesus' voice consistently surprised and challenged me. Jesus, as our conversations evolved, was a compassionate friend and teacher, who understood me enough to challenge me at a deep level.

Now, after returning home, I can't use that technique. The image of Jesus in that little boy on the New Delhi sidewalk is so vivid for me; I can't envision Jesus being anything but impatient with my comparatively minor cares.

When my spiritual director Ken and I realize what is going on, I can laugh at myself. I feel a little like Sister Tureeya. I can talk a good line about grace, but can I allow myself to receive it?

Once I name what is happening, I am able to reclaim Jesus as my wise, compassionate friend, without losing sight of Jesus who stands blocking the sidewalk, refusing to let me turn away. Until the next week, of course, when I need to stop once again to remind myself that Jesus can hold both grace and challenge, even when I can't.

✳ AFTERWARD ✳
In Celebration of Open Spirits

MY SABBATICAL TRIP TO INDIA in 2008 laid the groundwork for a new ministry at my church, Edwards Church, United Church of Christ, in Framingham, Massachusetts. In 2011, when a nursery school that had been renting one of our buildings closed, we began to dream of using the space in a new way. We paid attention to the growing interest in spiritual practices in our congregation. We took note of the fact that our campus was already used by a Jewish group, a Buddhist temple, an ecumenical Catholic Community, and a Pentecostal church. We also listened to our sense that there are so many people in the wider community yearning for spiritual nourishment who do not, for whatever reason, seek it in organized, traditional faith communities.

We began to imagine a place where people of all faiths—and people not identified with any faith tradition—could gather, create community, and seek spiritual nourishment. By the next year, Open Spirit:

A Place of Hope, Health & Harmony was born. We offer yoga classes, Tai Chi and Qi Gong, and meditation groups. We create interfaith book discussions and conversations about healing. We hold compassionate cooking classes, reiki events, programs to nourish public school teachers and empower challenged students, and events that seek to heal our relationship with the earth.

Many of the components of Open Spirit resonate with my learnings from my week at Jeevan-Dhara. Open Spirit is committed to exploring the connection between energy, spirit and healing—the connection I sensed so powerfully in that old healer in Rishikesh. Open Spirit honors the power of interfaith engagement, especially at the level of real people living out their faith—a power at the heart of the Christian-Hindu ashram movement, at least as it was intended. Most of all, Open Spirit is a celebration of the rich, joyous, painful complexity of being human and being in community.

I write this book in honor of the people of Edwards Church and the community forming around Open Spirit, in gratitude for the openness of their spirits, in hope that this new model may bring people together and offer healing for our world.

✻